Em Rusciano is a writer, comedian, and singer who is known for her performances on *Australia Idol*, her podcasts, her sold-out stand-up shows around the country, and for winning the 'Most Annoying Person' award at her Year 12 graduation ceremony. She collects owl figurines (157 of them to be exact), as a child wanted to marry Kevin Arnold from *The Wonder Years*, and can't stand the sound of people chewing. Em hopes to one day reside in a large house on a hill, have thirty-four dogs, and live exclusively on cheese and gin. She may or may not have already made a start on that last part.

Visit her website for less interesting facts:
www.emrusciano.com.au

EM RUSCIANO

Try Hard

Tales from the life of a needy overachiever

SIMON &
SCHUSTER

London · New York · Sydney · Toronto · New Delhi

A CBS COMPANY

TRY HARD – TALES FROM THE LIFE OF A NEEDY OVERACHIEVER
First published in Australia in 2016 by
Simon & Schuster (Australia) Pty Limited
Suite 19A, Level 1, Building C, 450 Miller Street, Cammeray, NSW 2062

10 9 8 7 6 5 4 3 2 1

A CBS Company
Sydney New York London Toronto New Delhi
Visit our website at www.simonandschuster.com.au

National Library of Australia Cataloguing-in-Publication entry
Creator: Rusciano, Em, author.
Title: Try Hard/Em Rusciano.
ISBN: 9781925310757 (paperback)
                9781925310764 (ebook)
Subjects: Rusciano, Em.
                Women comedians – Australia – Biography.
                Entertainers – Australia – Biography.
Dewey Number: 792.7028092

Cover design: Christabella Designs
Cover photograph by Mark Lobo
Typeset by Midland Typesetters, Australia
Printed and bound in Australia by Griffin Press

FSC
www.fsc.org
MIX
Paper from
responsible sources
FSC® C009448

The paper this book is printed on is
certified against the Forest Stewardship
Council® Standards. Griffin Press holds
FSC chain of custody certification
SGS-COC-005088. FSC promotes
environmentally responsible, socially
beneficial and economically viable
management of the world's forests.

For Denise Arline Spence
of Berrigan NSW

Contents

Introduction

W hy hello there!
Well done you on choosing to come on
this adventure with me. I can't guarantee you
well-constructed sentences, rational thought patterns or
the meaning of life, but I can promise you excess body hair,
foul language and wondrous tales of ridiculous behaviour
fuelled by a bottomless pit of anxiety.

I'm grateful for whatever has brought you here. Maybe
you know me from my stand-up comedy concerts, listened
to me on the radio or perhaps you watched me being rejected
by the nation on *Australian Idol* in 2004. You may be a fan of
celesbian (celebrity + lesbian) model-slash-actress-slash-DJ

Ruby Rose, forgot your glasses, saw my book, and thought you were buying hers.

Whatever the case, you're welcome here.

This is a safe space. I want you to snuggle down, switch off and find comfort in the fact that you'll leave this book feeling much better about yourself. Expect to mutter things like 'I'm so glad I'm not her,' and 'I'm nowhere near that neurotic,' and 'Why is she incapable of keeping track of her menstrual cycle?' during the course of our time together.

I only ask one thing of you: that you suspend all judgement from here on out. I'm going to take you deep; we're now explorers on a quest to find out how the hot, ridiculous mess that is Em Rusciano came to be that way. I also promise that is the only time I will refer to myself in the third person.

First an explanation of the title I've chosen for this book. I've been a try hard since the age of two. I attempted to give up being a try hard during the nineties, when it was cool to look like you'd slept in your clothes for a week, however I relapsed at the age of seventeen upon meeting the head of my gay mafia, Lyndon. It should be noted that only in Australia is 'trying hard' considered a derogatory and unappealing personality trait. In America they have parades for people who try hard. They give out medals and celebrate public holidays for humans who put maximum effort into everything they do. Here it makes you a loser, a tall poppy, someone who must be cut down and put back in their place. Remember the inspirational story of Kurt

Introduction

Fearnley? The Australian paralympian who *crawled* the treacherous 96-kilometre Kokoda Track? I bet – sitting in a pub somewhere in Australia – a group of blokes caught that story on the news and one of them probably shouted, 'Bloody try hard.' Yes, he did, fictional group of blokes. YES HE DID! What a champion.

I wonder why the act of putting in effort makes some people nervous? Just being me is an effort, can you even begin to imagine? I must try hard, *at everything*!

Of course, there are two types of try hards. One puts in contrived effort in an attempt to be something they're not and the other fronts up to everything, wanting to give it a red hot crack, with all that they've got. I'm only dealing with the latter. In my adult life, the trying hard has not lessened. If anything, it's increased, so I've decided to try and reclaim the term and make it a positive thing.

Writing and finishing this book was an enormous milestone for me for the following reason: when I was eleven I was asked to stand up in front of my class and spell the word Australia. You need to know that even now, I struggle to write my own name correctly; that part of my brain is missing, the spelling part. Obviously, I shat on the honour of my country's name and misspelled it in front of thirty-two other children. From memory I think I threw a Z in there for some inexplicable reason. After my classmates had finished laughing hysterically, my teacher then openly mocked me and said, among other unkind things, that I should know how to spell the name of the place where I live. I remember the sting of my eyes filling with hot rage tears and desperately hoping that the floor would open up and swallow me whole. It was one of my darkest hours. My teacher wasn't finished with me, she then took me aside after class and told me that my writing and spelling needed work, that I was on the cusp of high school and while obviously I would never be a writer, I did need to know how to spell and scribe simple words so that I could make something of myself. Remember, this was the late eighties – teachers could still tell you the painful truth without consequence.

Not to be too dramatic about it, but that teacher crushed me, she stomped her sensible shoes all over my creative spirit. The truth is, up until that point I'd been an avid storyteller. It hadn't occurred to me that how words were arranged and looked mattered. I just put them together in a way that worked for me and seemed to entertain my parents when they read them. My bedroom was full of notebooks filled with the wild tales I'd make up instead of doing actual school work. I also loved reading and dreamed of someday being just like Judy Blume, Enid Blyton and Roald Dahl.

But I stopped inventing stories after that incident.

It took many, many years for me to share my writing again. In fact, it wasn't until Twitter came around, and the editor of the website Mamamia, Mia Freedman, told me she thought I should start writing articles. She said that she loved the way I put words together in my tweets and that I should have a crack at a putting a few more words together

4

in the form of an article. This made my heart soar – could I be a writer again? Soon, though, the insecurities of my youth came back to haunt me. No, I probably couldn't, as I sometimes had to draw pictures of words to be able to spell them. I couldn't possibly do this professionally, I desperately wanted to but no. The public would surely think me a serial killer upon reading my strangely constructed sentences. When I explained the whole spelling/grammar situation to Mia, she said she had magic wizards to fix the mistakes before my columns were unleashed on the world and, well, that was that!

Now, here I bloody am! Writing! An entire book! I've gone and done this thing, I wrote every word, not a ghost writer in sight. Even though I like the sound of having a ghost write my book. But you know, that's not what that means, though rest assured, if it was, I would've been all up in that situation.

Coming up next we have the foreword written by my best friend in the whole world, Michael Lucas. We've known each other since we were eleven, we met at the infectious diseases hospital where our mothers worked at. He and I are each halves of the same person, I firmly believe that. The main difference being that he's an actual writer. I mean, he studied it and knows the correct placement of a semi-colon and wouldn't be caught dead using a double negative. He writes TV shows like *Offspring*, *Party Tricks* and *Wentworth*. Enjoy the next few pages for you are in the hands of the master.

After that, strap in.

This is one of the best things I've ever made that isn't alive. I'm proud of it.

I hope you love it sick.

Your pal,

Em

Foreword

Parents in the late eighties and early nineties weren't big on hiring babysitters. When heading out for a work function, armed with a pouch of tobacco and a bottle or two of riesling, they'd simply throw together a couple of random kids (generally linked only by their parents' workplace) and leave them with a twenty-dollar bill, a VHS rental of *Total Recall*, and the numbers for emergency services and take-away pizza. It was eighties parenting, and it was glorious.

I was a pudgy, gentle, uncoordinated mummy's boy who was perpetually anxious about the kids I'd face on those long, isolated, pre-internet evenings. Some nights, I'd be wedged with monosyllabic boys who farted symphonically and called me a 'spaz' when it became apparent I didn't know how to play *Mortal Kombat*. Other nights, I'd meet strange, slightly scary kids with names like Kane, who knew the location of all their parents' hidden sex toys, and were keen to provide a guided tour. But then one night when I was eleven, I was deposited with Emelia Rusciano.

Em was loud. She was brash. She was freckled. She called her parents by their first names when they were embarrassing her. She looked like Punky Brewster, filtered with Madonna, in the body of a sports nerd. She was as Italian as hot salami in a school lunchbox, and as white bogan as John Farnham's golden mullet. She could deliver word-perfect quotes of every Olympia Dukakis line in *Steel Magnolias*. She could smash a family-size pizza. She could Vogue. In short, she was everything a nerdy, pop culture-obsessed pre-gay could ever wish for. And I knew at once our couch time would become a sacred ritual.

The pre-teen Em really knew how to fashion a couch for *ultimate* comfort. At a pinch, she would procure supplementary pillows from the bed in a dedicated mission to construct a veritable Taj Mahal of cushion bliss. We would thoroughly nestle in, get a VHS rolling, pour cups of Fanta, place remote controls and the Dolly Doctor columns at arm's reach . . . and the conversations would begin.

The Em that I'd chat to for hour upon hour on those nights, caught between childhood and adolescence, was very much the Em who radiates out across innumerable platforms today. No filters. No judgement. She'd swing from giddy dissections of pop culture to brutally honest observations. We'd be laughing hysterically, then we'd be fighting back tears. We'd divulge dreams, crushes, tragedies. And we'd ponder a dizzying array of questions about our future.

Would Em ever get breasts? Yes. Briefly.

Would we ever lose our virginity? Yes, but not for a helluva long time and it would unfortunately be nothing like *90210*.

Would we know love? Heartbreak? Glory? Failure? Tick. Tick. Tick. Tick.

Would we stay friends? Would we fight? Would we find our way back to each other? Yes. Always.

Would Em ever realise that 'Material Girl' was about capitalism not about fabric? Not till a random conversation in 2015, no.

A quarter of a century has now elapsed, but always we've found our way back to the couches. It was on a couch that I watched Em weep, struggling to steer her way through post-natal depression. We were side by side on a couch when I blurted out that I had a crush on a boy. When we've endured our worst failures, when it's felt like the whole universe (or at the very least half the Twitterverse) was laughing at us, the couches have caught our fall.

I'm happy to report we actually own the couches now. And the drink of choice is more shiraz than Fanta. And Em has not only lost her virginity, she's managed to breed not one but two actual human beings. The eldest looks eerily like the Em I first met, but she's much more sensible. Chella will sometimes sit on the armchair beside us with earphones in, tapping at an iPad, seemingly disinterested ... but I'd like to think she's secretly listening in. I'd like to think she considers us bawdy and hilarious and soulful. But, more realistically, I'd like to think that she understands that all this, all the pouring out of hearts, the singing of Whitney, the interrogation, the togetherness, it's not a pit stop. It's not killing time before life kicks in – this is life. The stuff of life. The best of life.

You'd think that, after all this time, after establishing myself as the Barbara Hershey to Em's Bette Midler, and after consciously planning to spend our autumn years on the couch armed with gin and turbans, I could pithily summarise the woman Em's become, but I can't. I can't distil her. She's somehow fiercely maternal and yet still a truculent teenager. She has all the insecurity of a person who spends entire nights awake, racked with self-doubt, and all the confidence of a woman who can talk about discharge on the stage of the Palais. She's a proud feminist but that doesn't mean she's not taping the royal wedding. She can lose herself absolutely in the least convincing fantasy movie, but she can also deliver the most bracing of reality checks. It'd take a book to cover it all, so thank God, she's delivered one.

What I can do, however, very confidently, is recommend some reading conditions.

Foreword

Of course I'm gonna suggest you find a couch. You're gonna need one where you can lay flat out. I'd suggest you supplement the existing cushions with other pillows if needs be. It's okay if you wanna have YouTube on standby, cos God knows Em doesn't have an attention span either. I'd advise you to pour a red. Get some carbs. Nestle in. What follows is silly and sacred. Bawdy and heartfelt. The stuff of life.

Michael Lucas

1

The Epiphany

My life has been a series of unexpected, sometimes unbelievable, right-hand turns. Any time I've even remotely attempted to plan or control any aspect of what happens, life laughs at me and flicks up a killer curve ball. I've learned to roll with it, as resisting was causing far too much heartache. I went from athletic child prodigy to party girl to motherhood to *Australian Idol* to radio to TV to stand-up comedy and now here I sit, writing these words for you, and to say that the last thirty-seven years have been a rollercoaster would be an understatement of gigantic proportions and kind of gross. Sorry for using such an overworked phrase, especially considering my reality-TV background. Hey, at least I didn't whip out 'the pointy end of the competition' or God forbid go anywhere near using 'surreal' as an adjective. I've been working furiously hard since well, I could say since I was voted off *Australian Idol*, however it would be accurate to say that I've been working furiously hard since I came shooting out of my mother's birth canal on 1 March 1979! I'm not in possession of a slow down or an off switch, I'm in constant motion and, as you can probably imagine, that produces a shitload of energy: positive and negative.

I didn't set out to be a performer, although looking back, I suppose the signs that a life of professional showing-off awaited me were there. It only hit me very recently, twelve years after I started down this path, that this is what I do now, that being a comic, singer, writer and story-teller is my full-time adult job. The epiphany came when my manager Andrew called to let me know that I'd been invited to perform on the prestigious Oxfam comedy gala. I was absolutely beside myself. I'd grown up watching the gala and never once dared to dream that I would one day be on stage, at The Palais Theatre, doing stand-up comedy. The gala is – besides a way to raise much needed funds for the legends at Oxfam – a preview of some of the acts that will perform in the Melbourne International Comedy Festival (MICF). If you get to perform on it, and do well, it usually equates to a boost in ticket sales.

In comedy, there are generally two types of perfor-mances: you may do your whole solo show, which could run for sixty to ninety minutes, or you can do a spot. Spots are anywhere from two minutes to up to half an hour long, a megamix of your best gear usually performed in rapid fire in a line-up of other comics. Most comedians are brilliant at spots, it's their bread and butter, they flit from room to room busting out their highlights reel without a care in the world. I am fucking terrible at spots. This is a known thing. I fall apart. It is a horrendous, sparkly trainwreck. I just can't get my head around them. I need an hour to tell a story, to build to a finale – I need time to get to know my audience!

The Oxfam comedy gala required just seven minutes of my A game.

Oh. Boy.

On the day, I arrived six hours early, you know, because that is a completely sensible thing to do. Later I learned that the seasoned campaigners get there about an hour before they're due to go on. I set myself up in the communal dressing room and went about slowly driving myself insane with self-doubt. I roamed the aisles of the Palais hoping to absorb excellence from the blood, sweat and tears left behind by performers past. You know: The Rolling Stones, Lou Reed, Eartha Kitt, Bob Hope, and Abbott and Costello.

Other comics were filtering in and out for their tech runs. I, of course, obsessively watched everyone's dress rehearsal, comparing myself to the typically brilliant and well seasoned comics on stage. When I did my own soundcheck, I spent a great portion of it apologising for even being there. I kept looking over my shoulder expecting one of the producers to approach me, tap on their clipboard and say 'Oh dear, there has been a mistake. You should not be here.' Yes indeed, my imposter syndrome was off both its tits that day. After the soundcheck, my dad, Vincie, went out to move his car and realised that the battery was flat. Not wanting to be trapped in St Kilda when we were done at around 11pm, he decided that he would get a jump-start from someone, drive his car home, swap cars with Mum and then get back in time for our set.

Here is how that conversation between the two of us went down:

Dad: 'Em, the car has a flat battery, I just tried to start it. I am going to get a jump and drive it back to Eltham, swap cars and then come back here.'

Em: 'NO.'

Dad: 'What do you mean no? We'll be stuck here otherwise.'

Em: 'NO.'

Dad: 'I'll be back in plenty of time. It's three thirty now, it'll take me an hour to get home, that's four thirty, I'll swap cars and be back on the road by four forty-five, then back here by no later than six! We're not on until ten!'

Em: 'NO!'

Are you sensing a theme yet? There was no way I was going to let my father out of my sight. He was also being completely unrealistic about the time it would take for him to get to and from the Palais. It was a Friday night, he had to cross town, battle the infamous Punt Road, get onto the Eastern Freeway and back again. There was also footy traffic to contend with. In perfect traffic conditions that would be a ninety-minute round trip. On a Friday night, you could get to Perth and back in less time! He was my guitarist for the evening and while I wasn't sure I could tell the jokes, I knew I could sing the songs. If all else failed, I could sing, and Dad was integral to that so I didn't want to be separated from him.

Dad: 'See you in a few hours.'

Em: 'DAD, NO!'

After Dad abandoned me, I was approached by one of the shows' producers, who was keen to know what I'd planned on wearing for my performance. Wardrobe? I could do that! I showed her my ensemble of choice (a red-sequinned unitard with rainbow tail feathers and gold shoulder pads) and she told me I couldn't wear it because 'it wouldn't translate well on television'.

What does that even mean?! I looked at her and confirmed we were looking at the same fabulous outfit. 'Not translate well on television'? I think it would have translated fucking splendidly! She strongly discouraged me several times more and asked if I had another outfit. My only other option was a long red dress I happened to have in my suitcase. Just a boring old frock that I wore when I did corporate events. You see, I don't like performing in my civilian clothes, I like there to be a very distinctive line between Stage Em and Real-life Em. Stage Em is fierce, confident and capable! My sequins are like my cape, my mask, my lightsaber. On show days I suit up and Stage Em takes over – it's my ritual. I apply drag queen-level make-up, stick on my eyelashes, then step into the sequins. So my second mistake of the day was not sticking to my guns re: costume. I stupidly let them talk me out of my usual performance attire; I wanted them to like me, I didn't want to be perceived as difficult, so I went along with it. Imagine someone saying to Elvis, 'Sorry, babes, that white jumpsuit doesn't work for us, here's a nice black suit for you to pop on.' Elvis would be all like, 'I don't think so, darlin', eat a bag of dicks. I'm suiting up!' Obviously I am no Elvis but you get the gist.

Note to reader: I wish I could promise you that my analogies will improve over the course of the book, I *wish* I could.

Finally the other comics began to arrive, along with my third mistake of the day.

I decided it would be a great idea to sit with them and listen to them talk shit, run gags, gossip and reminisce about the times they or other comedians had bombed at this event. As I sat there, my brain was screaming, 'Abort! Abort! Leave this space immediately!' however my body was transfixed. Hearing them bounce gags off each other with such ease was incredible/terrifying. All I could think was: *I don't do those type of jokes! I don't deliver pithy one liners, nor do I make particularly witty observations and I certainly don't*

18

have any political statements to make! I tell stories about my family and sing songs with my dad.

It was about that time that my fourth mistake showed up. I decided that I should probably have a drink to calm my nerves. The only alcohol available was beer because: Australian comedy scene. I never drink beer, it makes me gassy and bloated. Still, for some unknown reason, I sat with the dudes and chugged beer. Sure enough my stupid, corporate red dress was becoming increasingly tighter as my stomach filled with gas (see, if I'd stuck with my usual attire my stomach could've expanded as it saw fit – sequined lycra moves with you, not against!). Finally my body could take no more and I had an excuse to leave the pit of testosterone in which I was residing. The other thing you need to know is that I become a needy dickhead when I get around those guys. I'm so desperate for their approval. I also have the sneaking suspicion that they don't take me seriously, that I'm considered a cabaret performer illegally infiltrating the world of comedy. That I hide behind my singing and costumes to cover the fact that I'm not very good at the stand-up game. I've no proof of this, of course, just an overall vibe. Yes, I know that's completely irrational and not an effective way to substantiate a theory. It still doesn't change the fact that when I'm around them, I over compensate, I go in too hard, I laugh a little too loudly, I also apparently *drink beer*, for fuck's sake.

You should also know that the obsessive calls to my father to check his progress and whereabouts had begun.

I would say I was on a ten-minute rotation. After about an hour, Dad obviously got sick of my harassment and TURNED HIS PHONE OFF, but in my mind, he'd definitely had a car accident and was lying in a gutter somewhere, bleeding internally, guitar smashed to pieces. I swear I worried about the guitar after first thinking about him, I can promise you that. Sort of. At worst they were simultaneous concerns!

Shall we recap where Em was mentally by 5pm?

1. Arrives six hours early.
2. Dad leaves to change cars over.
3. Gets talked into not wearing usual costume.
4. Sits in room with other comics who make her question her entire being.
5. Drinks beer, gets sick from drinking beer.
6. Dad's phone is now off and Em is convinced he will not be returning.

GOOD TIMES, Y'ALL!

At 6pm I was called into make-up and as I sat in the chair and looked at myself in the mirror for the first time that day, I noticed that the top half of my mouth looked as though I'd been punched or aggressively injected with some lip fillers. Do you know what I'd gone and done? I'd managed to manifest a cold sore in one day with special thanks to my anxiety! Yes! Face herpes roughly the size of Saturn hours before I was due on the telly. The make-up lady recoiled when she saw the angry white pustules on my lip. I was afraid she was going to send me away, and she would obviously have to set fire to her entire kit once my face was painted. I completely understood her hesitation. She began working on my head and I tried to focus, to clear my mind of all doubt and prepare to kick arse when I hit that stage in four hours' time.

When she was done I looked in the mirror and instantly felt better. I had my game face on, and slowly but surely small threads of confidence started seeping into my sweaty body. Sure I didn't have my costume, the ability to perform a stand-up spot or my guitarist: but I had my war paint in place and that would have to do. By this time it was 6.45pm and just as I was about to call the police to locate my father, in he walked with food and non-alcoholic drinks! Bless that man, he knew I would be in a state and not eating or drinking anything sensible. So Dad and I sat quietly in a room making small talk and I began to feel a lot better. I told myself that I'd earned this spot. My entire MICF run had already sold out before it had even started! All twenty-three shows were completely full – I was the only comic out of five hundred who had managed to do that. I'd worked bloody hard on my show, *The Motherload*, and since there were no more tickets left this would be the only taste the rest of Melbourne would get of it, and the first time the rest of Australia would see it, so I'd better make my spot seven minutes of heaven.

One by one the other performers did their sets until finally, after six hours of waiting, it was my turn. Dad and

I stood side of stage as a comic named Puddles the Clown sang a sad song. I took that time to do my pre-performance ritual. I closed my eyes and imagined my Nana sitting down in the front row, adjusting the brooch on her cardigan. I pictured my Uncle Haydn standing in a river fishing, giving me a thumbs up, and my Grandfather Ted seated at the head of the dinner table thumping it with his huge hands, which was what he did when he thought something was amusing. I pictured my Nono Luigi sitting on his porch, slowly waving at me, and my Nonna in her chair in front of the fan, smiling, peeling oranges. Why do I imagine all the people that I love who are now dead (spoiler alert) before I perform? Yeah, that's a fair question. I do it because it reminds me of what's important, it quietens the crap in my head and focuses me down to that one moment. It reminds me that this is just a job, that I have those people with and in me and that I can do anything.

Then my dear pal Joel Creasey, who was hosting the evening having just walked out of the jungle from his time on *I'm a Celebrity . . . Get Me Out of Here!*, introduced me. I looked at Dad, and was momentarily struck by how far he and I had come. How just a few short years ago I was unemployed and living with him, how as a kid he and I had sat together and watched this very broadcast, never imagining that we would one day be on it. How so many things had contributed to that person about to walk out on stage and perform in front of three thousand people.

The Epiphany

So here we are, here you are, about to discover the colours in the painting that make up the slightly blurred picture that I am. How did my spot go? Well, you'll just have to wait until the end of the book to find out, or you know ... skip ahead, but that would be a total dickhead move because I've put a lot of work into the chapters you are considering skipping, so don't, 'kay?

PROMISE ME!

It's time to take it back, all the way back.

Engage flashback montage music, possibly a harp or in the style of *Wayne's World*: *Doodleadoo doodleadoo doodleadoo doodleadoo doodleadoo doodleadoo doodleadoo doodleadoo* ...

2

The Miss Sheila Fancypants School of Dance

I suspect I was conceived during an episode of the eighties smash hit dance show *Solid Gold*. Sure, it started in 1980, a year after my birth, however let's not let actual facts stand in the way of my excellent theory. There can be no other explanation for the way I've turned out. Of course, I could easily confirm this with Mum and Dad but eww! No, please no, and why ruin the magic? I can tell you that thirty-seven years on I'm still the talk of the Greensborough Hospital maternity ward. Legend has it that after my mother gave her final push I arrived in full side-split position, jazz hands blazing, wearing my umbilical cord as a bustier.

I was born for lycra, aggressive pelvic thrusting and ferocious high kicks. At the age of two I started dancing at the local community church. The classes were run by a group of well-meaning senior ladies. I remember the room we danced in smelling heavily of Tweed, Ponds Moisturiser and Vogue Menthol Slims. I suspect a great deal of our choreography was borrowed from the aquarobics classes the ladies took at the leisure centre thrice weekly.

I would also put regular concerts on for my family. Not just Mum and Dad – oh no, my Aunty Jo had the misfortune of only living a few minutes away so she'd be made to make the journey up our hill to be an audience member, too. I'd line the kitchen chairs up thirty centimetres from my 'performance space', AKA an old piece of grey lino I'd found under the house. My dolls were always front row as they were my favourite kind of audience: their eyes were sewn open thus rendering them physically incapable of missing a moment of my masterpiece. Rest assured, if I could have done the same thing to my family members, I one hundred per cent would have. Mum and Dad would reluctantly shuffle in and I'd take my opening position as my pink ghetto blaster sprang to life. I have vivid memories of gyrating and body rolling to Alannah Myles's 'Black Velvet' in a totally inappropriate manner, barking at anyone who dared to break my drilling, unflinching eye contact. Upon reflection, my father would often look rather uncomfortable at my showings. I just assumed he was dealing with inner conflict about holding his obviously talented and

gifted child back from realising her full potential. I forgot
to mention my costumes usually involved my undies being
pulled up very high (think *Aerobics Oz Style*), tucked into
a bikini top, thirty-six plastic bead necklaces and a slick
of blue eye shadow across my lids. At the time I thought
these performances were the highlight of my parents' lives,
but now . . .

Now that I'm a parent, oh GOD. When my girls
announce they have 'something to show me' I know it's
either a DIY rock eisteddfod or nits. Quite frankly I would
prefer it to be the latter, as I can kill those. Although, my
youngest daughter has started placing a glass of wine next
to my seat pre-show, because she knows her audience.

By nine I was basically instructing all my classes and it was
becoming frightfully obvious (to me) that I needed more of
a challenge. I desired a hardcore *Fame*-style dance school.
I imagined studios with buckets of water suspended above
them so that the *Flashdance* training montage could be re-
enacted should the mood strike. My mother was dispatched
to find such an establishment and after some extensive
research (in the community *Yellow Pages*) she enrolled me
in the Miss Sheila Fancypants School of Dance.

It is at this point I wish to state that I attended a couple
of dance schools in my time, and I've combined a few of
my teachers into one and changed the names to protect the

guilty, but rest assured, the tales I have to tell have threads of truth sewn in. I'm sitting here cackling to myself about the 'threads of truth' line. I was going to go with 'integrity cotton' but I think that sounds like a church-funded sanitary product line.

The hall in which I danced was in a remote town miles from where we lived. It was the kind of place you would go to dump a dead body should the occasion call for it. In hindsight, the Miss Sheila Fancypants School of Dance could not have been in a more appropriate setting.

It was clear from the get-go that Miss Sheila passionately hated children. She didn't try to hide that fact either. Imagine Margaret Thatcher as a sinewy, bitter, gin-soaked ex-dancer, throw in a touch of the Dark Lord and you're halfway there. Why Miss Sheila chose a job that required her to work with small people day in, day out, still remains a mystery to me. In my opinion she was more suited to a career as a maximum security prison guard, a forensic entomologist or perhaps the manager of a slaughterhouse.

The week before my first class was to start at the Miss Sheila Fancypants School of Dance, a list of class uniform rules arrived in the mail. They were addressed to me and were in a silver hi-gloss envelope with MSFSD embossed on the back.

1. No jewellery.
2. Hair tied back into a bun.
3. Black leotard.

4. Pink ballet tights.
5. Pink ballet slippers with ribbons trimmed.
6. Black wrap cardigan permitted on cooler days.
7. Late comers WILL NOT be admitted to class.

Mum and I arrived fifteen minutes before the class started as instructed and were careful not to make any noise in the foyer – the humungous SILENCE sign served as a stark warning. Parents were not permitted to stay in the hall, however they were generously allowed to wait in the car park if their child was under the age of five.

Some children may have been frightened by such stringent rules, but not me, no ma'am. I knew that kind of Gestapo-esque approach meant I was in the right place. If my mother would have been willing to send me to North Korea to learn dancing, I would now still be living in Pyongyang, forcing my Kim Jong-un inspired flat top into a shapely bun.

I entered the hall with the other newbies. The seasoned children were huddled in the corner stretching and occupying as little space as possible so as not to draw attention. I yearned to join them. I looked around, eager to see my new leader. I needed confirmation that I was in the right place and when Miss Sheila stalked into the room, eyes narrowed, hair scraped back into a militant bun and a spine you could set your watch to, I breathed a sigh of relief.

She looked directly into my soul and barked, 'You there, suck that stomach in at once. We are not hippos, we are ballerinas! Back straight and tuck your bottom in or it will come to an unfortunate end. What are your feet doing? Toes OUT and stand in first position unless I tell you otherwise.'

I was home.

Sheila's brother Tim played all the accompaniment for us on a decrepit upright piano. It had seen better days and sadly, so had Tim. Sheila and Tim lived together in a flat above the studio. No-one had ever been up there. I imagine it was styled in an impending-nuclear-holocaust-bunker kind of way. Tim was obsessed with leopard print so I'm hoping a little of that was allowed in their flat. They had a cranky tabby cat called Barry (short for Baryshnikov) who would spit and hiss at us from the top of the stairs.

Tim was a lovely man, an immaculate, well-dressed bachelor. However, he was the wrong side of eighty; truth be told, he was the wrong side of dead. Sometimes Tim wouldn't hear Sheila's cues and by sometimes I mean Tim never once ever heard Sheila's cues.

Sheila took to violently whacking a large, glitter-covered stick on the top of the piano to let her brother know when to stop playing. This scared the living shit out of him *every time*, which is the last thing you want to do to a borderline incontinent senior citizen.

It went something like this:

Sheila: 'And five, six, seven, eight. Kick ball change. NO! Just KILL me now, why don't you? Why must you insult the art of contemporary dance in such a way? What did it ever do to you? Again!'

As Sheila abused us Tim would continue bashing out a cheery rendition of 'Let Me Entertain You'.

'Tim! Tim, stop playing. STOP IT, TIM!' *WHACK.*

Tim: 'Christ, Sheils [his nickname for Sheila, which she HATED]! I didn't hear you!'

I still have nightmares about the sparkling stick of misery. The glitter did nothing to make it less terrifying. I'm surprised Tim only had the three mini strokes he did during my time at Miss Sheila Fancypants School of Dance. Mini stroke number two caused Tim's hands to get stuck on a C-major chord and become immovable claws. It took the poor old thing sliding off his velvet leopard print-covered stool (hands still firmly stuck in playing position) to get Sheila to stop yelling at him and whacking the piano. I'm grateful she didn't poke Tim with the shiny stick once she realised what had happened and by grateful, I mean surprised.

The Miss Sheila Fancypants School of Dance annual concert extravaganza made the Super Bowl halftime show look like a kinder Christmas pageant.

We spent first term preparing for our RAD (Royal Academy of Dance) exams and then the rest of the year was dedicated to the academy's major production. Solos were up for grabs and we all took that shit serious as cancer. Sheila knew how precious those solos were to us and hung them over our heads like the sword of Damocles. Just because you had a solo bestowed upon you one week didn't mean it was yours for keeps. If you did anything to displease Sheila in the lead-up to the concert, you would have the performance ripped away, costume and all. One year Emma Davis had her solo as Odette from *Swan Lake* taken from her a week out from the concert. Her crime? Turning up to class with a hole in her stockings. Rookie error. Her mother had spent hundreds of hours hand-sewing white beads onto the bodice of the costume. She had painstakingly applied feathers to the delicate tutu and constructed a spectacular head piece involving diamantes and pipe cleaners; it was a work of art. I'm glad I wasn't there when she was told Emma had lost the solo, as I suspect tears may have been shed.

My mother still speaks in emotional tones of having to front up to 'costume inspection' where you not dare make eye contact with Miss Sheila as she went over your offering with a fine-toothed comb. If one seam, sequin or rosette was out of place she would yell, 'Not good enough!' and the poor mother would scurry off to try to fix the offending stitch.

After three years at the MSFSD, I was finally invited to audition for a solo. We were doing an all-singing, all-dancing rendition of 'It's a Hard Knock Life' and 'Tomorrow' from *Annie* as our closing number at the end-of-year performance. Friends, I probably don't need to tell you that I wanted the role of Annie worse than Kris Jenner wants North West's first sex scandal to happen at her place.

I begged Mum to let me get a spiral perm and a red dye job so that I could go method on that shit. I was prepared to live as Annie, in an orphanage, eating hot mush, just so Sheila could see my commitment.

On the day of the audition, I wore Mum's chequered apron, my old school shoes and had slept with foam worms in my hair to achieve a white girl 'fro. I had also spent a significant amount of time sussing out my main competition. I was leaving nothing to chance. My first rival was a girl named Selina who was Sheila's little gimp, a total suck. Selina had three pet rabbits, was a junior wildlife warrior and, I suspect, owned a large collection of yarn dolls. Selina always got a solo – her dancing wasn't even that great. Her body rolls lacked soul and her splits pizazz, if you asked me. Another girl, Charlene, who had an unfortunate lisp, was as keen as I was to land the lead role. Charlene had mad dance skillz no doubt, but due to the aforementioned speech impediment situation, I felt I had the edge on her due to all the speaking that would be involved.

I walked into the hall clutching the sheet music for 'Tomorrow' and handed it to Tim. Sheila entered the hall, whacked the piano and Tim began the intro. I was only a few bars in when the music morphed into one awful long mashed note being played over and over again, do you think that stopped me?

Nope.

I continued with my audition for a few more bars, however Tim was really starting to piss me off, he just kept playing that one loud note involving all the keys. I finally looked over and saw him slumped over the piano. Do you remember how many mini strokes Tim had during my time at the Miss Sheila Fancypants School of Dance? Yep, this was numero three happening right in the middle of my fucking audition! I looked over at Sheila to see if she'd noticed her brother was not well, and she hadn't. I had a choice to make here, friends, did I keep going to ensure I scored the role or alert Sheila to Tim's condition?

Forgive me, I kept going.

As I got towards the end of the song, Sheila finally realised things were awry in the soundtrack department.

'Tim! Tim, what are you doing? That sounds awful.'

She walked around the piano and realised that her elder brother was stroking out and managed to grab him as he slid off the stool.

Did I stop there? No way, bitches, I was going to finish that song no matter what. I had curled my hair, for goodness sake! After I'd hit the money note at the end of the song, I looked over to see Sheila cradling Tim in her arms. She was staring at me and I wasn't sure if she was offended or impressed that I'd pushed on.

'Selina! SELINA!' Sheila screamed out to the foyer.

Selina appeared from the wall, *Terminator Two: Judgment Day*-style: 'Yes, Miss Sheila? What do you need?'

'Please call the hospital and tell them Tim has had another episode.' Only Sheila could reduce a possible transient ischaemic attack to an 'episode'. She then turned her attention back to me and said, 'I couldn't hear a lot of that due to Tim's playing. You were very loud, I'll give you that. I think a spot in the chorus will do you.'

To this day I can't remember feeling so crushed at a rejection – and I was voted out by the nation on *Australian Idol* in 2004. The worst part was that rat-face Selina got the role. She ended up going to the hospital with Tim and sitting with him while Sheila finished her classes for the day. That bitch would have done anything to get the lead role, including enduring an eighty-six-year-old man shitting on her arm. You see, Tim lost control of his bowels in the ambulance. I heard Selina didn't even flinch. I'm sure she just sat there, stoic, gently singing, 'Tomorrow'.

I left the Miss Sheila Fancypants School of Dance after that end-of-year performance, for many reasons. The main being my mother couldn't handle the stress involved any more. I hear Sheila is still terrifying young dancers to this day and this makes me tremendously happy. She's a dying breed, Sheils, a teacher who has managed to transcend all the workplace-safety, verbal-assault and child-pandering rules that slow so many in her profession down. Occasionally, kids need to be terrified into submission, it builds character!

3

Doiymo

I spent the first thirteen years of my life in a little town called Diamond Creek or, as it is affectionately known, Doiymo. Doiymo is about forty-five minutes north-east of Melbourne. It had the vibe of a country town, even though it wasn't that far from the city. We lived in the ritzy part of Doiymo, literally on the right side of the tracks. The train line divided the town into two very distinct neighbourhoods. The Doiymo East kids were as rough as you like, and I suspect the movie *Boyz n the Hood* starring Ice Cube took a lot of its inspiration from the mean streets of DC East. We lived on the hilly side of the train station, on tree-lined streets. The air was softer and warmer up our end.

Everyone knew everyone; we had street barbecues and games of backyard cricket. I'm pretty sure the Doiymo East kids just threw stones at cars, rode around on broken down BMXs and lived in tents.

We also had the Diamond Creek pool on our side. My Aunty Jo worked there, and that gave me HUGE social status cred. I could take my friends there, not pay to get in and get free Sunnyboys! Aunty Jo is one of my mum's younger sisters. Whenever I would get in trouble at home (which was often) I'd escape down to her place for time out and all the junk food I could handle. Her pantry was full of sugary treats and WHITE BREAD. Something we weren't allowed at home; just the fresh wog food at our place. My kids aren't allowed it now either. Yes, you were right, Mum – there I said it! On our side of Doiymo we also had the milk bar, where $1 bought you a bag of lollies the size of your head, and the world famous Binishell.

I must stop now and reflect on what was an impressive yet ultimately flawed feat of modern architecture. The Binishell in Diamond Creek was built in 1979 and named after Dr Dante Bini, who came up with this particular construction technique. A huge dome-shaped balloon was inflated and then a layer of concrete was poured on top of it. Once the concrete was set, the balloon was deflated and removed. Look, obviously there was a bit more to it involving steel beams, mesh and reinforcement but you're not here for architectural accuracy so let's move on. Basically we're talking about a massive egg-shaped multi-purpose hall.

In the Binishell I played netball with my mum, attended the Diamond Creek town fair bake-sale and also went to an underage disco. Why our little town was picked for basically the only structure of its kind in all of Victoria (as far as I know) remains a mystery to me.

It had to be pulled down years later as a couple of other Australian Binis had large chunks of concrete fall from their ceilings. I remember some fairly severe cracking in the Doiymo one as well. It was demolished at our town fair in 1991.

My favourite fact about the town in which I grew up is how it got its name. Legend has it that a farmer, who was presumably quite influential, lost his prize heifer in the creek that runs through the town. He was apparently devastated, so much so that he named the entire place in her honour. While some suburbs are named after lords and ladies or perhaps a famous explorer, the place where I grew up was named to pay homage to a dead animal. I attended Diamond Creek Primary School, which was only a short walk from my house. The school colours were brown and yellow, AKA poo and wee, which would be shouted at us each week by the opposing school at interschool sports. Bat tennis could get pretty brutal back then, let me tell you. However, it was our school emblem I really think you'll all appreciate. The outline of a yellow diamond sat atop our left breast, some squiggly lines representing the creek inside of it, a tree was there too and just in the middle of the squiggly creek lines, underneath the tree, was DIAMOND THE COW TAKING HER LAST BREATH! Yes, my primary school's logo was our town's namesake drowning in a creek! It only dawned on me in adulthood how bizarre that choice of emblem was.

Imagine that first P&C meeting.

President parent: 'Okay everyone, we need to decide on a school emblem. I was thinking maybe a eucalyptus leaf, some wattle or perhaps a kangaroo?'

Parent 2 (possibly a descendent of the farmer who founded the town): 'What about a large mammal partly submerged in water, facing its impending death, in the creek that runs near the school?'

President parent: 'I like it! Nothing says nurturing learning environment for small children like a drowning cow!'

The Doiymo primary school uniform is also the reason I started barracking for the Hawthorn Football Club in 1985. I saw them on the telly and thought, *HEY! I wear those colours! We're the same! I'm going to love them now because we wear the same colours!* That philosophy worked out pretty well for me as the HFC went on to win the '86, '88, '89 and '91 VFL grand finals. I couldn't believe my luck! I came to passionately love the players; my favourites were Jason Dunstall, John Platten, Dermott Brereton, Chris Langford and Michael Tuck. I traded VFL cards like a demon, I was a cut-throat wheeler dealer back then. I kept them wrapped in foil in my *Ninja Turtles* bumbag and at recess we'd all congregate under the library to commence the day's trading. Back in those days, the Lockett/Platten Brownlow card was the Holy Grail.

My family lived on Collins Street, which was on the same street as the cop shop and when us kids would walk past it on the way home from school, we'd always stand a little taller and talk in hushed tones, just in case the cops were going to sting us for being delinquent, slouched-over, loud-talking hoodlums. My kinder was also on that street, so obviously it was the happening part of town. Our place was at the top of the hill and everyone knew it because of the cubby house that sat in the front yard.

It was mission brown with white trimming and had EMY written in very large white capital letters across the top. My dad and Uncle Bruce had built it especially for me. By the by, Emy is what my family call me, it was also what I was called for most of school. 'Emelia' was reserved for my Nana and when I was in trouble with my parents. 'Em' came much later in my career.

When I was five, something deeply upsetting happened to that cubby house, in fact, I think I can pinpoint the exact moment my relationship with my parents started to go sour to this one incident. I loved that cubby, it was all mine, I could do whatever I wanted in there and put up whichever curtains I pleased and no one could tell me 'NO, Emy, your dancing leotard cannot be the table-cloth', or 'Orange cordial and gold sequins don't mix'. My cubby house was the scene for many dramatic readings and performances, it's where I went to clear my head and meditate on the day's activities. I wrote on the walls, used it as my location to cut Ken's head off when he was caught cheating on Barbie with Skipper, and it had a pile of squashed ants and spiders in the corner, which I had taken out with my plastic princess heels. Reading back over that last paragraph makes me sound like a future serial killer, doesn't it? If we had a check list, I think I just achieved bingo!

Then on 1 October 1981, my sister Abby went and got herself born. I was almost three years old and even now I still remember feeling slightly confused as to what all the fuss was about. Sure, she was cute and small but I was doing some pretty epic finger painting at kinder so, you know, we all had things going on. When she came home from the hospital with Mum it quickly became obvious that Abby was now the favourite and the cat and I had been relegated to annoying novelties. Still, I got on with things, I continued to model my personal style on Punky Brewster, ate a shit-ton of Kraft Singles on Saladas and was generally an epic legend.

Abby got older and started following me around everywhere as little sisters are prone to do. Mum was a fan of the home haircuts back then so Abby and I were soldiers fighting together on that front. Parents don't do that any more, do they? I know kids who have their own Instagram accounts just dedicated to their locks and hairdressers. In *my day*, Mum would come at us with a pair of nail scissors and a mixing bowl with horrifying results. Don't worry,

I'll put a few in the photo section, yes, you can skip ahead now and look, I'll wait.

Abby and I found a way to co-exist and by that I mean she endured being bossed around to within an inch of her life. I eventually let her join my crew, which consisted of our neighbours (an English brother/sister combo: Sarah and Adam) who lived two doors up, and my cat Fluffy and me. One pleasant autumn afternoon, with the last vestiges of the sun on my back, I came home from school and saw something that still, to this very moment, burns a deep hole in my soul. As I got out of the car after a stressful day of home-corner duties, stale pasta-mural making and nature-table assembling, I noticed that something had changed about my cubby. Now, I was no reading expert, but I was pretty sure another word had been added UNDERNEATH MY OWN NAME ON THE FRONT OF MY CUBBY! You guys, this is not a drill. As I walked towards it with both hands firmly planted on my five-year-old hips, I saw very clearly that someone had besmirched my beloved cubby house with white paint. That *someone* had written 'and ABBY' under my name on the front of *my* cubby house.

To say I flew into a rage would be an understatement of Herculean proportions. I lost my shit big time. Hadn't she taken enough? My room, my old clothes, the love and affection of my parents? I simply couldn't believe it. Something in me died that day and a deep chasm formed in my soul – no, I am NOT being dramatic! I walked over

43

to the cubby, pointed at my sister's name and shouted 'No!' to the universe.

It took me weeks to be able to even look Dad in the eye after I found out he had been the one to add my sister's name to my property.

I had mistakenly thought we were bros, he and I. Turns out he was just a traitorous whore available only to carry out my mother's bidding. Yes, it had been Mum's idea, but *he* had carried out the unforgivable act. I was devastated for weeks. I refused to speak to either of my parents. While writing this chapter, I asked Mum if she remembers my utter devastation at this event. She said she didn't realise it had upset me so much! That she was just trying to get me and Abby to play together, that she had meant no harm by defacing my beloved headquarters.

Whatever, *Jenni*!

Dad knew how deeply the action had wounded me and in an attempt to make it up to me, he constructed a bike from scratch. It had a sissy bar, a black glittery seat and streamers in the handle bars. He painted it black and white and I would cruise the streets of Doiymo like a badass mofo. I would ride to my Aunty Jo's house – she lived down the bottom of our hill behind the Anglican church. I hung out with her sons, my cousins David and Thomas, a fair bit back then. They were quite a few years younger and both the devil incarnate but other than my English neighbours, pickings were slim. Rest assured they've both grown into lovely young men, however as

44

kids, they dressed in Batman costumes, set things on fire and threw themselves off the tops of houses while you were babysitting them.

Vincie's attitude to safety back then was lax at best – if you are a product of eighties' parenting then you'll remember. The eighties was the decade where standards slipped a whole bunch. Mums were going to work, dads didn't quite realise that, and kids benefitted from and took full advantage of the distinct lack of supervision. I remember roaming the streets with my wicked awesome bike gang (read: David, Thomas and the Brits) for hours at a time. The only thing I had to protect me was my Stackhat with giant drawn-on eyes to scare away the aggressive magpies that lived in my area. I wouldn't speak to my parents for the entire day! The only way they could contact me was if I was at my mate's house and they happened to call at the right time or if I was near the public pay phone on our street – sometimes we'd answer it when it rang but most of the times we ignored it.

I vividly recall being on a bean bag in the back of a car that didn't have a back seat and my sister being in a Moses basket in the boot. All the windows were up and I'm pretty sure someone was smoking. Come to think of it, I reckon a few West Coast Coolers were involved in this scenario too! We had a rusty swing set that was definitely tetanus ridden, and the front legs of the frame would launch off the ground as you swung higher and higher. Not only was that encouraged by my dad, we started timing our airtime and keeping a record of it. We regularly flipped the entire set.

If you knew how to dial 000 you were old enough to babysit. On more than one occasion I drove on my father's lap to the shops, not just up the driveway but the whole way to the Doiymo Tucker Bag! SPF 2 was considered over-the-top sunscreen protection and 'because I said so' was a valid and accepted answer for any request denied.

To prove that this book isn't just an elaborate way of getting back at Jenni and Vincie for their parenting deci-sions in the eighties, I will now celebrate one of the greatest ones they ever made.

In 1987 I had both a musical epiphany and a sexual awakening. My mum's youngest sister Rachael was staying with us and she had bought some records at Brashes before she arrived. (Side thought: Was there a greater gift than a Brashes voucher in the late eighties?) One of these vinyls was a record by the name of *Whispering Jack* ... If you didn't automatically add in a self-echo when you read 'Jack' then I'm not sure I can love you.

I'll let you take a moment.

I'll let the waves of emotional emotion sweep over you.

I'll let you imagine John Peter Farnham's feathery light wispy blond hair cascading over his ears. (Which he always liked to hide the top of as he was self-conscious about them. Only the hardcore fans know that bit of trivia.) I loved the album cover because it had a large black and white picture of JPF whispering into some bitch-who-wasn't-me's ear.

I can't believe that woman isn't a household name; if I'd had John Peter Farnham's mouth that close to my face I would have shouted it from the rooftops. Some people are ungrateful dickheads, aren't they?

The best part about the album was it had all the words to all the songs printed on the inside of the cover – I could sing along straightaway. Of course I learned every word by heart and also knew that I needed to somehow become John Peter Farnham's child bride. While watching *Hey Hey It's Saturday* one night I heard Molly Meldrum announce that John would be touring the country, that there was to be a *Whispering Jack* performance in my home town! The venue? The Melbourne Sports and Entertainment Centre. Back when venues used what they were in their title. Oh, the Melbourne Sports and Entertainment Centre, that must have sports and entertainment. Now it's names like the Westpac Centre, which sounds like a psychiatric facility for bank workers, and Hisense Arena – what the fuck is a Hisense? A flower show? Feminine hygiene products?

I began my campaign for tickets. They were about $50 and in eighties money that was roughly the equivalent of $1000. I asked Dad every day – he was my best bet. I was appealing to another musician, to someone who knew the power of music and how important it was to see it live. Dad was probably still feeling bad about the cubby situation, so he agreed to take me along to see my future husband.

I remember on the day of the concert I went to school completely convinced that I would never return. I said tearful goodbyes to my pals for the last time as I knew that John would see me in the crowd that evening and take me backstage to aggressively hold hands with him. He would beg me to tour the country with him, and I would have to give up my Grade 3 schooling and live my life on the road. That was a sacrifice I was willing to make, such was the depth of my love for him.

My outfit was paramount to my success in luring JPF. On my feet I wore a pair of white leather scrunch-down boots with fringing along the side and silver studs across the front. On my legs I wore a pair of white cotton stockings with a low hanging gusset as I had grown considerably since the previous winter. Can you think of anything that sits so close to your vagina that is less appealing than the word gusset? There was another slight problem with my tights: the black, coarse hairs on my legs were shooting through the holes in the material. I spent a large portion of my preparation time trimming them with my Crayola craft safety scissors, which was like trying to take to the Amazon jungle with a pair of nose hair trimmers. I popped on a homemade rara skirt that Mum had whipped up out of dancing costume offcuts and an old parachute jacket of hers. A white T-shirt with fringing and studs (to tie in with the boots, obviously) topped the skirt and for warmth, I wore my mother's Jenny Kee for Coogi cardigan, which had sheep on the back and cotton balls stuck on the front. My hair had been swept up into a high side ponytail, held in place with a scrunchie purchased at

Kleins. I KNOW. Do you even remember that place, how good was it? You could get a genuine string of pearls for $9.95 and if you were lucky enough to be offered a scratchy you could get up to fifteen per cent off those bad boys! Sadly there is no photographic evidence of this night, Mum says that I was in such a rush to leave I wouldn't allow a single photo.

Hopefully my words have painted a vivid enough picture for you.

Dad and I caught the train in from Doiymo Station. Usually that would require a knife-proof vest but not that night! That night the Farnesy Army had our backs.

We got into the entertainment centre and I just remember feeling as though I would burst with excitement. I couldn't believe that I would be in the same room, breathing the same air as my hero John Farnham. The audience was a sea of desperate thirty-five-year-old women in high-waisted Levi 501s and tight spiral perms, my dad and me.

I was legit the only kid there. Vincie let me purchase a program and a Chiko Roll and we went to sit in the hall and wait for the show to start. As I was poring over the program, everything went dark. Then, a scary man's voice starting saying, 'Pressure, pressure, pressure . . .' I knew EXACTLY the song he was about to sing and I told everyone is a 56-row radius about it.

'IT'S "TAKE THE PRESSURE DOWN"!'

Then the sheer purple curtain dropped and there he was. No-one in that room loved him more than me in that moment. I stood on my seat and sang along as loudly as I could.

It was euphoric. I was eight years old and in a room with thousands of other people who worshipped at the altar of John Peter Farhnam and for one night only we had our sexy, microphone stand-twirling messiah within arm's reach. It was a utopia I never wanted to leave. I looked around at the signs, the ciggie lighters being waved in the air and the happy faces, and it felt like home. The rest of the band was there, I knew them all! David Hirschfelder was on keytar, Angus Burchall on drums, and Venetta Fields, Laurie Fields (not related or married) and Lisa Edwards on backing vocals.

JPF rolled out all the hits. It was almost too much to bear – and then it happened. A man with a bagpipe and a kilt appeared on stage and he began to play a song I consider our country's rightful national anthem. The entire room realised we were about to bear witness to 'You're the Voice' and shit got real, fast. Everyone was up out of their seats, hands on hearts and many with tears streaming down their faces. I was definitely having some kind of religious experience. I sung so hard, I hit every high note, I thought my heart would explode in my chest. It truly was one of the greatest moments of my life, one of those defining experiences that never leaves you. Then it was over.

Dad had to sit through me reliving the concert all the way home. There was a singalong in the carriage as well. I wasn't even disappointed that John Peter Farnham didn't spot me in the crowd and ask me to marry him on the spot. I really wanted to go to school the next day and tell everyone about it, so it all worked out for the best.

Around the time of my sexual awakening and the Farnham experience, I also started attending Diamond Valley Little Athletics. Not to be too much of a wanker about it, but I was a gun. I could flat-out run and jump and hurdle, and each Saturday I would roll up in my thin red Bonds T-shirt, my black bloomers, my pulled-up white tube socks and my Puma Darts ready for action. When you win everything in an individual sport such as athletics, attending is super fun! I would take out the McDonald's Achievement Award most weeks and most weeks be forced to give it away as my mother refused to let us eat there. At the time I thought that was a huge injustice, however now I'm eternally grateful to Jenni for putting her foot down where fast food was concerned.

My first year in Little Athletics I broke the record in all the sprint events and the jumps, and each year, as I moved up an age group, I would go about taking out most of those records too. I was somewhat of a legend at that club. I decided very early on that I was going to be an Olympic athlete – my heroes were Flo-Jo and Carl Lewis – and by the time I was ten I was already the best high jumper in the country. I competed in my first national championships at

51

the age of nine – can you believe it? I had been selected in the Victorian team to compete in the under 10 girls high jump. I wasn't particularly tall but I had mad hops (that's street talk for 'could jump very high'). My principal, Mr Goodger, had gotten wind that I was competing in the national championships so he organised a fundraiser to help my parents cover the costs. A special newsletter was sent out (the highest of honours) asking all the kids to bring their spare coins to school the next day. When I arrived I saw that our art teacher had drawn a huge picture in chalk on the basketball courts of me high jumping and all the kids were instructed to fill the picture up with their coins! How lovely is that? It took all morning but by recess the whole drawing had been covered with one, two, five, ten, twenty and fifty cent coins.

By the time I was twelve, athletics completely formed my identity. I had all the national and Olympic qualifying times stuck up on my walls and forced my parents into finding me a coach. He was a lovely Irish man by the name of Tom Kelly; I had decided that I was going to be a sprint hurdler and had researched the best coach in my area – Tom was that and then some. Tom looked after me, and he did his best to calm my raw energy and anxiety. Looking back, I must have been exhausting for him. I was a precocious little shit and he was the perfect match for me. I absolutely adored him. Tom passed away in tragic circumstances in 2014, and one of my biggest regrets was not finding him as an adult and thanking him for all he did for me.

I've been extremely lucky in the way of coaches; when I left Tom I was coached by a legend by the name of Kathy Lee. She dealt with me at a time when I was a teenager, in huge conflict with myself and my parents, and gave me a reason to turn up somewhere each day.

At around thirteen I started to hang out with the other elite junior athletes. Future Olympian and Commonwealth games legend Tamsyn Lewis was one of my aths besties. She matched my level of competitiveness and love for our sport on every level. It was a relief to find people as obsessed as I was – I didn't have to hide my encyclopaedic knowledge of all the current and past world records. While I wasn't all that popular at school, I was at the track; the other athletes became my family. When I was fourteen I was selected to go and stay at the Australian Institute of Sport to be part of the Sydney Olympic development squad. We were to say there for a week and be tested by the coaches and scientists to see if we had the goods to go all the way. We arrived in Canberra and were shown around the AIS, and as soon as I got there I knew that's where I wanted to be. I would do whatever it took to get myself a scholarship so that I could live there and train full time. A lot of my friends had come up with me and I was rooming with my pal Anna Deery (who will feature later when I lose my virginity . . . *not* to her but she was there).

After our first night I got up super early and went over to the track. I wanted to get an early session in and was hoping to see one of my favourite Australian athletes training as well.

I wasn't disappointed. As I jogged around the track I noticed a woman in the shot put ring. I slowed down to see if I recognised her and OH MY GOD it was one of my all-time favourite Aussie athletes. The lawyers have made me take her name out because they think she'll object to my upcoming description of her bum. I highly doubt it but I have obeyed their wishes. She was obviously doing a bit of strength work for her throwing events. As I got closer I noticed something else: she was doing shot put in what looked like – well, it looked like a g-string! I'm guessing her black bloomers had just gone up her crack, but to me, at the time, my hero was in her undies, in a deep squat, five metres from me. She had a bottom like a ripe brown peach, the thin piece of black lycra cutting it square up the middle. That image has stayed with me for a very long time, even now I can see it as though it only happened this morning.

Athletics was my everything, it formed most of my identity, and there was just no doubt in my mind that I would go on to be an Olympian. The thing is, at the time, I never felt good enough. I didn't once stop to acknowledge all the wondrous things I was achieving. Looking back, I feel I owe that kid a huge apology. I want to honour her right now by saying to her (yes, me, a young me, stay in the moment!) that you were an elite athlete with incredible physical skills; no, you didn't make the Olympics as you'd always planned, but that doesn't matter. You came pretty close, you qualified for the World Junior Championships and had you not torn *both* your hamstrings competing in another sport – a sport that you had been banned from competing in by your coach but you did anyway – who knows what would have happened?

The thing is, you were enough, you were *more than enough*.

I'm sorry I appear to have something in my eyes . . .

What?

You want to know what happened, don't you? You want to know which sport I was illegally competing in and what happened to end my athletic career. It is *so* ridiculous and yet makes perfect sense that I went out in this fashion. Seriously, it's as though someone wrote this for a TV script.

What was it that ended my promising Olympic career?

One.

High.

Kick.

I was competing in the State High School Aerobics Championships, because of course I was. I had just competed in the Australian Pacific Athletics Championships and my body was on the edge. I was super fit and twitchy, which is when an athlete's muscles are most vulnerable. I went up for an aggressive high kick to the beat of 'Pump Up the Jam' and felt the rip in my hamstring instantly. As I crashed to the ground, the other went out under the stress. I'd torn my right leg's hammy and strained the left one. Everyone knows that once you tear a hamstring, especially as badly as I did (it was like a level 6778 grade tear) you never fully recover. I'd also been having problems with my spine; due to chronic hyperextension it had developed three stress fractures. My body was breaking down on me from severe overuse and that one high kick sent it over the edge. I tried to rehab my broken down body for a full year, I spent every day at the Victorian Institute of Sport gym in South Melbourne bouncing on a fucking fit ball, strengthening my core, doing everything except the one thing I wanted to do, which was run.

Finally it was decided by my coaches that I should perhaps try another sport, one that didn't stress my hammies out so much. Yeah, okay, you guys! It's not like my entire life had been geared towards this one sport and that my whole being was tied to it, let's just try something else, easy! Okay, so it kind of was. I switched to velodrome cycling and took to it very quickly. Turns out sprint cycling and track sprinting are very closely tied in terms of muscle groups. Did I even own a bike? No! So why not start riding one at high speeds down the cliff face of a velodrome with no brakes to speak of? In my first competition I came third in the Austral Wheel Race and third at the state champs in the 500 metre sprint. I know, how annoying.

Cycling was looking pretty promising, and then – well, then a certain person started working at the VIS gym. A certain person who would maybe put a baby in my guts and make cycling kind of hard. But let's not jump ahead of ourselves, there is still so much more ground to cover.

4

Third Generation Lunatic

To understand why I am the way I am, one doesn't need to look much further than the man who sired me. My small Italian father, Vincie, is a glorious lunatic and I wouldn't have him any other way. I truly don't know where to begin painting the picture of my dad, there are so many stories from growing up with the most impatient man in Australia. Imagine if Super Mario, George Costanza and Danny DeVito had a baby and you're almost there.

I think the reason I am so capable of a vast array of things is because as a kid, I had no other choice. I had exactly 2.5 seconds to complete a task my father had set or he would take it over, briskly moving me out of the way and berating me for being too slow. Not because he is a mean person – he is the kindest person I know – he just has zero tolerance for slowness! So be it Lego, putting Spokey Dokes on my bike or eating, it was kill or be killed with my dad. As a result, I'm an extremely quick learner and have crippling anxiety over the completion of menial tasks. Swings and roundabouts, eh?

My father is in constant motion, he is always busy, and a lot of the time, everything and everyone pisses him off. He is also charming, hilarious and generous. My dad and I have always been great mates, we're similar in a lot of ways and he has always amused me. We're both impatient and intolerant of the world in general. As far back as I can remember, Dad has made me laugh – but not always intentionally. He has a deep love of slapstick comedy, and as a kid I would sit with him watching Jerry Lewis movies. He'd call me into the lounge room most Sundays and make space for me next to him on the couch, enthusiastically telling me, 'You'll love this one!' My dad has a very particular way of sitting. He crosses his legs and then tucks his foot under like a pretzel. Everything coiled up like a spring, ready to explode at a moment's notice. When we'd watch Steve Martin, Billy Crystal or Chevy Case be ridiculous on screen his whole body would be locked in fits of giggles while his legs remained tightly crossed; tears streaming down his face as one of the actors would take hit after hit to their junk.

Dad moves around like a small hairy ninja. He makes no noise when he walks, it's quite something. Every night, once we were all in bed, he would dart from room to room checking everything was locked and secure. He'd do it with the speed of a hummingbird, and in tattered jocks that hung from his sinewy frame. The only giveaway was the click-clack of the locks, then the fridge would go as he'd grab one last olive before going to bed, but you'd never hear a footstep, not one.

Dad has always preferred to make stuff rather than buy it, which is fine unless you're the person who has to try to pass the item off to your friends. He made me everything from bikes to go-carts. He'd study the picture of whatever had taken my fancy and proclaim, 'I can make that for half the price, Em!' Then we would head down to the local hardware shop in Diamond Creek, sometimes a trip to the tip was required for spare parts, and then he would lock himself away in his garage, crazy-inventor style. His creations hardly ever looked like the picture, instead taking on a strange *Alice in Wonderland* Mad-Hatter-tea-party form of their own.

If I was to pin down the greatest insult involving the use of an inferior product to replace the thing I really wanted, we would need to take it all the way back to 1987. Just like any eight-year-old girl at the time, all I wanted in life was a Cabbage Patch Kid, the kind that came in the green box, with the woollen hair and the birth certificate with a ridiculous name like Cecilia Badelia written on it.

Picture it: Christmas Day, 1987.

I was ready.

I had written a *very* specific letter to Santa in red texta demanding one thing and one thing only: a Cabbage Patch Kid. I gave him no other options. There was no way he could stuff this up.

Dear Santa,
I just want a Cabbage Patch Kid this year, that is it.
I don't need anything else.
Please give the rest of my gifts to the children in Africa.
Here is my list:
1. Cabbage Patch Kid.
Thank you,
Emy Rusciano.

I woke up at 4am Christmas morning and waited – we had been told we couldn't get up before 6am, which I now think is very generous of my parents. Finally the hands on my Mickey Mouse watch reached the twelve and the six, and I sprang out of bed, shook my sister awake and bolted for the lounge room. The first thing that worried me was that there was a pile of presents from Santa, and I had been expecting just the one box. I knew that those dolls were very expensive, that's why I had specified that I only needed that one gift! Maybe I had been super, extra good that year? My sister was told to unwrap her gifts first, so I watched patiently as she unwrapped the My Child doll she'd asked for. Do you remember My Child dolls? Before the doll could become your one true kid and you its one true Mummy, you had to kiss it on the nose? They had those terrifying glass eyes and soft felt skin?

Then finally it was my turn. I headed for my pile and opened all the gifts that weren't Cabbage Patch Kid–sized. After a frantic three minutes of unwrapping I eventually got to the last gift. The first indicator that something was terribly wrong was that the last present was not in the shape of a box. It wasn't even *in* a box: it felt soft and it rustled. I was prepared to overlook this and assume there had been some sort of terrible box mishap at Santa's workshop. I tore the paper off and what I found was a plastic bag with a *fake*, thin, manky, wannabe Cabbage Patch Kid inside. I looked for the genuine birth certificate and all I found was a gel satchel that said, 'Do not eat.' I checked for the signature of the Cabbage Patch Kid inventor on its arse. In my heart of hearts I knew it wouldn't be there, there is no way Xavier Roberts would have put his name to this abomination. No signature, string hair and she didn't even have proper individually hand-stitched toes. She didn't even have toes, just a long webbed foot. Needless to say, I was beside myself. The injustice of the situation was too much for me to bear and what I did next I'm not proud of, but I feel 'Santa's' reckless behaviour led me to it.

I ripped my sister's My Child from her little hands and I KISSED ITS NOSE. I mean I really made out with it, I got that nose pregnant with my tongue.

Before she had.

I know. Was there a greater crime to commit against your younger sister in the late eighties than forcibly adopting their My Child through nose sexual assault?

To be fair to my parents, I did receive a real Cabbage Patch Kid two months later on my birthday. The dolls were expensive and they needed to spread it out over the two occasions. As a parent I totally get that now, but then . . . not so much!

Besides having a love of cheap knock-offs, my dad is also a talented self-taught musician. My earliest memories are of going down to Barwon Heads and Torquay on the west coast of Victoria to watch him play and sing with his band, Owen Yatemen's Big Fat Brass. Owen Yateman was a huge, tanned, slab of a man. He looked like the lost member of ZZ Top. Big Fat Brass were a pretty big deal at the time, Dad even got to play on a tour with Joe Cocker and Sammy Davis Jr. The Big Fat Brass's repertoire involved a great deal of *The Blues Brothers* soundtrack. I could recite every line in that movie and fiercely shake a tail feather by the time I was six years old. It's one of my dad's all-time favourite films, second only to *The Great Race* – Tony Curtis and his sparkly blue eyes never got old in our house. There is a very famous scene from *The Great Race*, where Max tells the professor it's time to 'rise and shine' after a night spent sleeping in the snow. The professor doesn't like that particular turn of phrase and cracks the shits with Max big time. It goes on for quite a bit. Almost every morning for the twelve years I attended school, my dad would act out that entire scene, playing all the parts himself, as he woke my sister and me.

Vincie is extremely mechanically minded. He started out as a fitting and turning apprentice and even won apprentice of the year in 1968! Dad has always loved trawling hard rubbish collections looking for abandoned electrical equipment to bring home and make his own. The thing is, once he has rebuilt something, only he knows how to work it. Rather than just one simple switch, his re-creations usually involve an elaborate series of manoeuvres. Turning on our home theatre system had more steps involved than launching a nuclear warhead. He controlled everything that plugged in or had a battery at our house.

Em: 'Daaaaad, I can't get the TV to work.'

Vincie: 'Just flip the silver switch, put it on AUX, hold down the red button, press the blue lever and wait 5 seconds.'

Vincie: [Waits 2.5 seconds] 'Is it working?'

Em: 'No.'

Dad: 'Here let me, you're hopeless.'

Dad has weighed sixty kilos since he was fifteen and not put a kilo on since despite being a massive feeder. Dad doesn't eat proper main meals, his life is spent grazing on his own antipasto creations. He keeps a cheese box in the fridge filled with pungent dairy – the salami is kept in there as well. Dad cooks for everyone else, though. Masses of lasagne, pasta and schnitzels. He loves feeding people, it's his way of showing love and care.

Dad is a mad keen F1 revhead; he is particularly passionate about Ferrari. Mum and he went on a trip to Italy and, against her better judgement, they ended up at the Ferarri testing track. He'd somehow gotten wind that they were testing the new Alonso and wanted to have a peek. Like that is something Ferrari would allow. Don't think that the massive security around Fiorano Circuit, so that people couldn't just have a peep at top-secret new models, put Dad off. Oh God, no, he made my mother crawl on her stomach under barbed wire just to catch a glimpse!

My father doesn't believe in hospitals or doctors – there's nothing Aspro and Savlon can't fix. Which leads me to this: the story about my father that has been seared into my memory for all of time.

I arrived home from school one spring afternoon to find my dad tinkering with our brand-new ride-on mower in his shed. (Although to call it a shed is a little insulting to the tool palace it actually was.) As soon as I saw the tiny red hood popped on the mower I began to panic.

'Dad! What are you doing?! That thing is brand new, you don't need to fix it. Just leave it alone, would you?' I shouted at him.

'No, Em, you don't get it. It's not powerful enough to make it up the side hill. I'm just making some slight adjust-ments. It needs a tad more juice, just a tad. Wait and see how fast it goes!' He was genuinely pumped at the prospect of his pimped-up mower.

'*Dad!* Why do you need a fast lawn mower? It's not like you're going to be racing it. Stop it. Does Mum know what you are doing?' This was my last resort, my one and only big move to attempt to control his behaviour – playing the Mum card.

'*No!* Don't you tell her either.'

As if.

'You're out of control. Have you even tried to make it up the hill? I'm sure it would, that's what it's made for!' I already knew the answer to this, as he wasn't one to trial things.

'I don't need to try it, Em, I can just *tell*. Just *trust* me, I know what I'm doing.'

I sighed heavily and went in to find my mother so I could dob on him and hopefully put a stop to this madness.

Luckily for him, Mum was still at work, so at fifteen I was the only responsible person in the house. I sat down to watch *The Afternoon Show* on the ABC and as the strains of *Degrassi Junior High* began playing, I heard what sounded like a V8 firing up. The people next door had just bought a brand-new Holden Clubsport so I thought nothing more of it until I saw my father *zoom* past the window at great pace on the ride-on mower.

Let's put the speed aside for one moment and discuss his choice of safety clothes, shall we? On his feet not steel-capped boots, runners or even shoes of any kind, just a pair of thin rubber thongs because that is my dad's standard issue footwear. He would scale a fucking volcano in thongs if given the choice. Dad has *huge* Hobbit toes, they account for fifty per cent of his foot length, and they can only roam free in an open-toed situation. He welds, mows, cuts, runs, does *everything* in thongs. Thongs aren't known as safety footwear, especially since his huge toes cause the toe straps on them to bust out continuously. He solves that issue by putting bread tags underneath the little knot that goes through the toe hole. They once caused him to fall off our roof. He was up there trying to increase the signal power of our aerial (of course he was) and one of his thongs got caught in a loose roof tile. I was in my room, heard an almighty thump on the roof and then saw him him sailing past my window, his oversized cargo shorts flapping in the breeze (everything is oversized on Dad as he is 5 foot 4), barefoot and screaming 'Faaaaaaaaark!' as he went.

I raced to the backyard to try to get him off the mower before he took himself out.

As I turned the corner I heard him start up the hill. I yelled out to him to slow down, but he just turned around and raised his fist in triumph as the mower made light work of the enormous hill at the side of our house. You see, in his mind, Dad was in his own personal grand prix. He continued to fist pump as he rode the mower in a very jaunty fashion. You've never seen someone so pleased with themselves. Up and up the mower climbed until – well, until everything went to shit.

The back wheels began to furiously spin, which caused the front wheels to lift off the ground, and suddenly the mower had flipped and Dad and the mower were rolling down the hill. He came to a stop just as the mower began somersaulting backwards down the hill – *still on*! I couldn't believe what I was seeing, Dad and the mower had become one and I didn't know how to stop it. I screamed for him to get out of the way as he flew off and the rogue machine catapulted towards him. Then, as I watched on in horror, the mower rolled over the top of his forearms. It was carnage.

Dad isn't one for blood and he went white when he noticed streams of it clumping and pooling in the vast amount of hair on his arms. I ran over to him and ripped my school jumper off to try and stem the tide. He kept muttering, 'It's just a scratch, I'm fine, Em.' Needless to say, it was far more than just a scratch. Thankfully the mower had ended its path of destruction after crashing into the side of a large tree.

That was also the moment Mum arrived home to find her eldest daughter cradling Vincie in her arms, covered in blood and freshly cut grass. But having been with my father for well over two decades at that point, she wasn't surprised. I remember her sighing and putting the shopping bags down, and bracing herself for the catastrophe she was about to witness.

As soon as we mentioned he would have to go to the hospital he began yelling at us.

'I am NOT going to a hospital, just get me the Savlon and an Aspro. GET ME THE SAVLON!'

Then he passed out.

Do you get it now?

Lunatic.

The thing I should tell you is that he isn't the original lunatic; that title goes to his father, my grandpa, Luigi Rusciano.

A couple of Sundays each month I would go with my dad and my sister and sometimes my mum to visit Nonna and Grandpa. They lived in a small, immaculate house in Coburg in Melbourne's inner north-west. Luigi served as a chef for the Italian army and I later found out was a secret vegetarian! Please understand that if you tell an Italian that you're a vegetarian, they will offer you the chicken instead of the lamb. He immigrated to Australia in the early fifties with his brothers, my father and my Nonna came over a short time after. About twelve years later my Aunty Josie was born. It has been hinted that my Grandmother suffered a couple of miscarriages and perhaps a stillbirth between the birth of my dad and my Aunty Josie, but it's not something that has ever been openly discussed. I can't even begin to imagine what she must have gone through being in a foreign country and having to suffer that kind of trauma.

Sundays were spent with Grandpa either picking his tomatoes, planting his tomatoes, attaching his tomatoes to a stake or drying his tomatoes. We were on a year-round cycle with the tomatoes. After we tended to the tomatoes we would go in and get ready for our lunch. Nonna made everything from scratch. We'd start with pizza and minestrone then came the pasta followed by schnitzel and salad. We ate the same thing every weekend and I never once grew tired of it. To this day (and believe me, I've searched), I've never tasted food as delicious as those Sunday meals at my grandparents' house.

Luigi never had a bank card and only ever dealt in cash. I got my first $50 when I was ten and it gradually grew from there. Every time I'd say ciao at the end of a Sunday visit he'd slip a wad of cash in my hand like we were taking part in an illicit drug deal. Obviously, I thought that was awesome beyond awesome.

Luigi once started a war with his local bakery. The Italians who had owned it decided to move on and sold it to another family, an Asian one. If you are related to or know an old-school immigrant you will also know their tolerance towards other races and religions is pretty low. I'd just stop short of calling them racist, *just*. When Grandpa realised that the bakery he had been going to for over thirty years was now run by another family, an Asian one, he started to find fault with the bread. (Note: there was nothing wrong with the bread.) He then accused them of hiding the 'good bread' in the back of the shop when they saw him coming. This situation escalated to a stand-off between Luigi and the baker. He refused to leave the shop until the 'good bread' was produced and tasted. My father was called into the shop on this occasion with the police not far behind.

I want you to understand how devoted my dad was to his father. After Nonna passed away, Dad began to take care of Luigi. He would call in each day and make sure he was okay. As time went on and Luigi needed more and more help, my father went above and beyond his duties as a son. He would work a nine-hour day then drive an hour to cook dinner for his dad, wash and shave him and then go home and cook dinner for him and Mum. If I achieve nothing else with this book I want to properly acknowledge my dad and his loving efforts with Luigi.

When it finally came time to move Grandpa into assisted living, I was relieved, as it gave my dad a much needed break.

Before you conjure up images of piss-infested carpets and green walls, rest assured, he lived in the Taj Mahal of nursing homes. Every flat surface had a plasma TV and they all got a wing-back recliner to watch the aforementioned plasmas in total comfort. Luigi would shuffle around the home unassisted, swearing at people in Italian but he did it with such charm no one really cared. As you can well imagine, in that environment, men over the age of eighty-five who don't need an adult nappy or a walking frame were a hot commodity. It's about a five-to-one ratio in there. Basically, he was living in the Playboy Mansion for seniors. Because he didn't have access to any cash to give me, he took to swiping small items from the kitchen to present me with when I visited him. He'd beckon me closer with his tiny, spindly hands, give me a knowing smile and pull from his pocket a small container of jam/honey/Vegemite. I love the idea of him conspiring all morning to steal them,

I also know a part of him wished he would get caught so that he could argue with someone. I'm not sure how good he was at stealth given he was in his late eighties – I think they had a fair idea where all the tiny packets of condiments were going.

Grandpa became increasingly tired of being in the nursing home, he wanted desperately to be out and about. It was hard for him to accept that his body was no longer able to do the things his mind wanted it to. He grew frail and eventually I noticed the light starting to leave his eyes. My visits would only elicit the briefest of smiles and then he'd go back to listlessly staring out the window. When he stopped wanting to get out of bed, Vincie and I knew it was time.

The night Luigi died I sat with him in his little room. The nurses had washed him and tucked him in bed, the skin on his face had relaxed and it was the first time I had ever seen my grandfather look still and at peace. I wandered around the room talking to him – I don't know why, I guess part of me still expected him to answer. Then I looked in his small wardrobe and found all his clothes neatly folded. Luigi was the *most* dapper dresser you have ever seen, his favourite look was a pair of well-ironed front-pleat Italian suit pants, a pair of leather loafers, a woollen cardigan, a Penguin polo and a Kangol cap.

I picked up one of his jumpers. It was a blue one, he always wore blue. Luigi was no fool, he knew it brought out the striking colour of his eyes. Those same blue eyes now look at me each day in the form of my youngest daughter. I held the jumper to my face, and it still smelled of him, a mixture of scents: mint, soap and olive oil. I felt wretchedly sad, he and I were kindred spirits – he got me and I got him. I was most upset for my dad, though. That was the hardest part, seeing my beloved Vincie broken over the death of his father. They'd had a complicated relationship, but Dad loved his father in a beautiful and honest way. He has never said much about what kind of a father Luigi was but I suspect he was a harsh one. I am certain he was not demonstrative in any way – he was a proud, angry man, my grandfather.

So there you have it, I am third-generation lunatic.

My dad is going to pop up a lot over the course of this book so I wanted you to have a better understanding of him. This is not to take anything away from my mother, she has had to endure us both for many years. Mum tends to behave in a normal fashion, so she hasn't provided as much fodder for this book. I'm very much a daddy's girl; the fact that he now tours the country with me playing guitar and not charging me for it is testament to that. How did he come to be doing touring with me? Well the truth is, in 2013, when I was an unemployed, thirty-five-year-old single mother and had just moved back in with Mum and Dad, my guitarist at the time up and moved to Canada.

Dad came into my bedroom one night and asked me what I thought I might do now that I didn't have a musician to play my shows with. I responded that I had no idea and then burst into tears. He gently said, 'Em, I thought maybe I could play guitar for you? I mean, I haven't played in twenty-five years but I'll practise. You won't have to pay me. Would that help you?'

YES, I KNOW! HE IS A FUCKING SAINT AND EVEN NOW I AM CRYING WRITING THIS.

And so he did, we did, and I have enjoyed every minute since. Dad retired from the place he worked at for thirty-five years and thought he would play a little golf and rewire a few flatscreen TVs. Instead he is spending it touring the country being hit on by women and drinking all the light beer he can handle, but more about that later.

5

A Hobbit with a Taste for Glitter

When I was thirteen, my family and I moved to a suburb in Melbourne's northeast called Warrandyte. Warrandyte circa 1992 is best described as a place where wealthy, geriatric hippies lived in treated-pine mansions. Their pastimes would typically include robust games of Trivial Pursuit, doing craft using the natural environment as their source material and tending to their own personal crops of marijuana. It was a peaceful, sleepy town where parents drank cask wine and favoured crystals over deodorant. Dreamcatchers outsold milk and bread two to one in Wazza.

The main drag in Warrandyte didn't offer much in the way of fun times. The highlight was a shop confusingly called Scandals Candles! I'm not quite sure how the scandal portion of the shop title came into play and to this day I question the need for the exclamation point. When I think of salacious acts, patchouli-scented tea lights don't exactly spring to mind. I refuse to believe it was purely for alliteration purposes. I like to think the owners poured hot wax on their genitals while chanting Satanic verses before crafting the candles they sold and that's what made them scandalous.

There was one clothing shop called River Clay that dealt exclusively in tie-dyed, hemp fisherman pants. They also had the monopoly on the lucrative dreamcatcher market. Not surprisingly the owner drove a new Mercedes. Our art gallery only ever displayed local handmade pottery: 'da Vinci da Sminchie! Have you seen this divine pinch pot Maria Skogal made from clay she found beneath her house?' We also had an organic health food shop (way before they were cool) that had twenty-three different types of herbal tea.

There certainly wasn't a lot for the youth of Warrandyte to do. As a teen there was no way to escape, there were only two buses that went in and out each day, and we never really knew when, as they seemed to operate on a schedule known only to the drivers. We had the Yarra River to frolic in during the warmer months; of course, that was if you didn't mind the odd brown snake whooshing past you on a rapid. I once spent a summer trying to smoke cedarwood-flavoured incense, I'd read that it promoted power and strength if you burned it, so imagine what smoking it would do for me! The pamphlet I'd seen in River Clay (of course that's where I'd purchased the incense sticks) did say to do it in a fort or castle with an army before battle but all I had was our chook shed. Sadly, it was sans chooks as there had been a massacre on Easter Sunday: a fox had literally got into the hen house and taken them all. To this day the incident is still referred to, among my family, in hushed tones and never within earshot of my mother, as The Great Easter Sunday Chook Massacre.

For me, the one huge bonus about moving to Warrandyte was the fact that the boy I was completely and somewhat disturbingly obsessed with lived only a street away. His name was Ryan – even typing his name now makes my heart race a little. His coolness factor was off the charts. He had blond hair that was styled similarly to Kurt Cobain's (who was hitting his peak at this time), amazing eyes, tanned skin, long, muscular limbs and could sing. His father drove a vintage Porsche. Ryan's hotness covered a three-grade radius. By that I mean the girls in the year below him, in his year and the one above were all in love with him. Obviously not that same love I felt, silly superficial bitches. My love was real and deep and belonged on *The Wonder Years* with Kevin Arnold and Winnie Cooper. One afternoon Ryan was running to catch the bus and as I watched him run, wondering what we'd call our kids, I noticed something fall from his backpack. I checked no-one was looking and I swooped in on it and to my absolute delight I saw that it was his deodorant. Something that had touched him! Something that *smelled like him*! For a small, apprentice stalker that was a jackpot. I shoved it in the front pocket of my backpack and quickly looked around to see if anyone had witnessed my desperate act. No-one had – the perfect crime! Yes, I accept I was one step away from knitting a yarn doll from our combined DNA.

There was just one thing standing between Ryan and me. One major roadblock souring our inevitable eternal love: MY BODY HAIR. By the age of thirteen I was essentially a hobbit with a taste for glitter. The stuff was growing everywhere, from the tops of my feet to the tips of my fingers. Can I ask, what possible evolutionary purpose is there for giving an thirteen-year-old girl hairy feet? Why did God smite me so? I'm not kidding, me emerging from the shower each morning was reminiscent of the opening scenes from *Gorillas in the Mist*. I had a snail trail you could plait and a fine set of hairy koala ears that hung out either side of my undies. Once the nipple hair arrived, the only smooth skin I possessed was the soles of my feet.

Oh yes, for any men who may be accidentally reading this book, we ladies get boob pubes or, as I like to call them, bubes. In my experience, that is the threshold most women will not cross with their partners. We will shit ourselves giving birth in front of you, allow you to stroke our hair as we delicately chunder, but you will *never* see our boob hair, that is our line in the sand.

I didn't know what to do about all the hair. My mother didn't tell me how to go about removing it as she is a blonde, blue-eyed, hairless Australian woman. I'm not even kidding – naked, she looks like a seal, not one goddamn hair on her body.

Needless to say, when my sports teacher told us that the school swimming carnival was coming up, I became catatonic with panic. I was in Year 7, and it would be the first time that we'd all see each other in our bathers. The stakes had never been higher, maximum hotness was required, so basically I was fucked. My classmates had no idea of the thick patches of hair I was unwittingly cultivating beneath my tartan kilt and cream cotton shirt. The date of the swimming carnival loomed large on the horizon. I went to bed thinking about it and I woke up thinking about it. I planned to fake being unwell to get out of going to school, and three days out I began complaining of a sore throat and headache. I had to plant the seeds of sickness well in advance if I had any hope of convincing my mother I was truly unwell come the day of the dreaded event. I didn't succeed, she called my bluff when I thought perhaps I could still go to athletics training, my only reason for existing at that point. 'If you're well enough to run, you're well enough to swim.' Tough love from my mother AKA the hairless wonder.

When the day arrived, I hadn't been able to do much deforestation. When I popped on my green speedos in the locker room, to my horror I noticed my armpit hair could no longer be tucked away and held in place with sweat and Impulse Merrily Musk. It looked like I had two guinea pigs nestling under each arm. As I desperately tried to rip them out with my bare hands, a girl named Rose walked into the locker room and looked straight at me. I couldn't get my pits in check in time and she caught a glimpse of the situation under my arms.

Reeling back in horror she exclaimed, 'OH MY GOD! THAT IS GROSS!'

I was mortified. Of all the people to see me of course it had to be her. Rose had the kind of tits that made watching her do the backstroke a religious experience. She had the body of a Playboy Playmate at thirteen. Her hotness knew no limits. She had a gap in her front teeth that made her look like Madonna and a very rich father who went to the Oscars for a film he'd worked on. The Year 12 boys wanted her as much as the Year 7 ones did. Oh, and probably the most poignant thing about her was that she was also Ryan's girlfriend because OF COURSE SHE FUCKING WAS.

Rose backed out of the locker room at an impressive pace and ran towards the pool. I didn't know what to do. I knew she'd be gathering an army, and as I stood alone and frightened in the dunnies I imagined her describing the black forest upon my person to every single judgemental teenager she came across. Rallying the troops against me, whipping them into a hormone fuelled frenzy. I sat paralysed with fear, waiting for the repercussions of Rose seeing my untamed body mane. Then, after ten or so minutes, I knew my fate. Over the loudspeaker I heard: 'Could Emy HAIRYano please report to the pool deck, your fifty-metre freestyle event is about to start. Emy HAIRYano.'

That brilliant bitch.

I wasn't even in the fifty-metres freestyle!

Needless to say, this incident pushed me over the edge. Not long after I found an old, rusty BIC razor of my dad's, locked myself in the bathroom and took to my legs. The thing is, I didn't know about lubrication before shaving. I hacked away at my red raw skin and removed most of the upper layer of my shin. Do you think the masses of blood pouring off my legs stopped me? Christ no, I thought that if I removed enough of the leg the hair could *never, ever* grow back. My knees didn't fare much better and then as I attempted my inner thigh, I slipped and cut it deeply. Look, I don't know how great your biology is but there is a pretty major artery running along your inner thigh. I realised things were getting out of hand when the first towel became saturated with blood. Long story short: I had to go to hospital and have my thigh sutured together with butterfly bandaids.

Unfortunately this wouldn't be the only trip to the emergency department involving attempted hair removal. I had become obsessed with finding ways to rid myself of my situation and on a food shopping expedition with my mum, I saw something called a Silkymit. I knew she wouldn't buy it for me so I stole it.

You see, on the packaging it promised to remove hair with just a few gentle strokes. I could do that! I was also relieved to have finally found an answer that didn't involve sharp edges or boiling hot wax. As I had the coverage of a large bear, I decided to go in with a more heavy-handed technique, upping the ante on the 'gentle strokes' and going more with an 'aggressive stabbing' motion. The result was not the silky smooth, hair-free body promised. The result was second-degree burns on my flaps and another trip to the hospital for some topical cream and light bandaging.

The other major issue I was having at this time, besides the body hair, was my menstrual cycle. It appeared to have a mind of its own and showed up whenever it damn well pleased. One afternoon in Year 8 science I felt a wet patch in my nether regions as I shifted in my seat. Naturally my first though was, *Oh God I've shat my pants.* We've all been there right, guys? *Guys?*

I gently raised myself up to inspect the damage and there on the back of my green and white striped uniform, to my pain and anguish, was the Japanese flag. It was horrific. It looked like a traffic accident involving a small animal had occurred on the bottom half of my school uniform. We're talking a level one, no-where-to-run blow-out. I felt betrayed by my vagina. I waited until everyone else had left the classroom and then quickly tied my jumper around my waist. I spent the rest of the day hiding in the girls' toilets. When the final bell rang it dawned on me that I needed to get myself to the bus bay and onto a bus home without anyone seeing the back of me. I was also troubled by the prospect of the beige-coloured faux velvet bus seats. I couldn't make any sort of contact with them or it would be clot-o-clock, if you know what I mean. You don't ever live down a period-stained school dress and you know it.

With my jumper and a lowered backpack acting as a shield over the large red stain, I kept my back to the wall as I made my way to the bus stop. I crab walked onto my bus, found a seat near the front and squatted above it. I had to be careful to make sure it looked like I was actually sitting and be equally as careful to not actually sit. TWENTY-FIVE MINUTES I STAYED IN THAT DEEP SQUAT. My legs were starting to violently shake as the bus pulled in to drop me off. Mercifully, I lived only fifty metres from the stop. The problem was Ryan (you know, only the love of my life) also got off at this stop and being the perfect human that he is, stood up and waited for me to get off first. This would have required me to walk past him which of course meant I ran the risk of SMEARING PERIOD BLOOD ON HIS LEG. Then I would be in front of him, which would leave the blow-out at the back possibly exposed. I just stared at him with wide, panicked eyes and shook my head like a carnival clown game. He smiled that glorious half-crooked smile at me, laughed and got off the bus. I waited until he was a safe distance away, then carefully manoeuvred myself down the steps all the while clenching my legs together to stem the overflow and waddled up my street. When I got home and inspected the damage there was nothing left to do but shower, fully clothed.

I lusted after Ryan for all of high school, but he never knew. I did eventually start dating his best friend, Clarke. Partly because Clarke was very cute but mostly because it put me one degree from the object of my intense affection. When I left the school, I didn't see Ryan for a long time, in fact we didn't have any contact until many years later. Let me see if I can recall the date . . . Sunday 27 February 2011. My daughters and I were at the movies, about to embark on a slaying of the classic *Romeo and Juliet* (*Gnomeo and Juliet*) and I heard someone say, 'Emy Rusciano.'

I think you know where I'm going with this.

IT WAS RYAN!

My God, so many thoughts and emotions. I'll try to give them to you in order:

1. Shit, I'm not wearing any make-up!
2. Oh, he looks amazing.

3. Damn, my children are here.
4. Shut up, you love your kids.
5. Yes but they make me seem unavailable.
6. You are unavailable you twat, you're married.
7. Shhh, brain, Ryan might hear you.
8. Wait, he's in a kids' movie. He must have kids.
9. Shit, he's married. So are you, remember?
10. Oh God, it's been too long I have to say something . . .

Em: 'Ryan! Wow, how did you know it was me?'

Oh *brilliant*, Em. Great opening line for the man you obsessed over for most of high school.

Ryan: 'I see you on the TV each week, it wasn't hard.'

Brain going into meltdown – he's been watching me on the TV?

Em: 'What? Really? You, um . . . watch TV? Of course you do . . . So . . . Oh . . . You've seen me on the TV.'

Mayday! Mayday! We're heading for a crash landing.

Ryan: 'Are these your girls?'

It took me a while to respond to this one, for ten seconds I was standing at the bus stop I had shared with him during high school. They were the greatest five minutes of each day.

Em: 'Oh, yes. This is Chella and Odie. Are you here with offspring also?'

Ryan: 'Yes, I've got two here and two on the way. This is my wife . . .'

Yes, he was an almost father of four. He had a lovely wife, they lived near where he and I grew up, they go to the movies together on Sundays and he hadn't aged *one day.*

The movie started and so of course I sat there analysing and agonising over the three-minute conversation we'd squeezed in. I had to make up for my atrocities when the lights came up so I started workshopping ideas.

I would ask about the impending birth to throw them off the fact I obviously still had a schoolgirl crush.

I would talk about my husband – YES, MY HUSBAND! Someone loves me now, that's right!

As the lights came up I steadied myself – I knew this had the potential to go horribly wrong. I needed this to end on witty banter at the very least.

We gathered up our respective children and walked slowly up the stairs.

This is it, Em, get it together . . . Nothing boring or inane . . . You need pizazz and brilliance . . .

However, as I looked at him with his two impossibly beautiful sons and glowingly pregnant wife who he obviously adored, I realised I was being ridiculous. What did I think was going to happen? I'd impress him so much he'd obviously want to go back in time and be my boyfriend? Because that's as far as I had got. I wanted him for my fourteen-year-old self – it wasn't practical for now.

Once I remembered I was in my thirties and not fourteen I was able to look at him through adult eyes and see that ship had well and truly sailed.

A Hobbit with a Taste for Glitter

In the end we talked about gestational diabetes and nappies, I gave him a kiss and a hug (swoon – look I'm only human, okay?) and I wished him all the best. When I got home I went to my glory box and finally threw that can of Lynx Africa in the bin.

6

Virgin Territory

After starting out life with such promise, genuine ability and high hopes, by seventeen I'd managed to bomb my Year 12 exams, not get into university and ruin my athletics career. My poor parents; instead of an educated Olympian they ended up with a broken-down teen working at the local pizza joint for $6.30 an hour 'under the table'. The restaurant – and I use that term loosely – was run by a huge Italian man named Mario. His mother worked in the kitchen, his father ran the front of house and his brothers waited tables. I was the only non-family member employed there and even then I suspect I was only hired because of my last name. It was a 'cash only' establishment, no-one wrote receipts and the staff car park looked like a luxury car dealership: Mario's brothers, who sometimes pretended to be waiters, drove Lamborghinis, their mother drove a Porsche and Mario had a late-model Ferrari. Dropping me off on Thursday, Friday and Saturday nights was the highlight of my dad's week, he loved being so close to that many expensive European cars. My duties included ensuring that each customer's meals had an extremely high salt content so the bar staff were kept busy, cleaning off the *paper* tablecloths after each table was vacated and reading out each and every order slowly to Mario's mother as she didn't read English. I'm not sure why they bothered having me read out the orders to her as she tended just to make whatever the hell she felt like on the night. Sometimes that coincided with what a patron had actually ordered and sometimes it didn't.

My employment at this fine Italian establishment came to an abrupt and somewhat dramatic end. One Monday morning, I arrived to pick up my little orange envelope of cash to find police tape covering the front door and some decorative bullet holes running along the back window. The fact that the chef and the two blokes who waited the tables all drove cars over the $100k mark had not escaped the police and ultimately the tax department. They were shut down for money laundering and suspected 'gang-related activity'; it made the local paper and everything.

My next part-time job was in retail at a shop delight-fully named Penetration – I'll let that one sink in, shall I?

Despite what the name may suggest, it genuinely was just a clothing shop, no latex or strawberry-scented strap-ons in sight. Being a naive seventeen-year-old, I didn't give the creep factor of the name much thought, until the phone calls started happening.

'Hello, Penetration, Emy speaking.'

Deep breathing.

'Hello, Penetration, this is Emy.'

Breathing gets faster, laboured . . . 'I'll penetrate you, love.'

Hangs up.

This was occurring about four times a day. The three other girls who worked there and I took turns blowing the whistle down the phone when calls of that nature would come in.

My boss – a terrifying man – owned the shop with his equally terrifying brother. I'd been there roughly four months when they turned up with our new uniform, which consisted of a tight white T-shirt and pink velour tracksuit pants that had the word –

Yes. Yes, they really did. You know where I'm going here, don't you?

The fluffy pink pants had the word 'Penetration' written across our arses. What the fuck? No.

I refused to wear the uniform and suddenly my hours were reduced to a sum total of none.

After that I became a swimming teacher. Paddling around in piss-infested water turned out to be far more pleasant than my other two jobs. Working at a public swimming pool exposes you to the dirty underbelly of humans trying to keep themselves clean; the things we would find in the dark crevices of the change rooms at the end of the day would make your eyes water. Also, nothing quite prepares you for the first time you see a public spa turned off at the end of a long day of use. When the gentle veil of bubbles stops the freaks come out: bandaids, scabs, hair – so much hair – and, inexplicably, condoms. Look, I'm no fertility expert but I'm fairly sure a condom would be rendered useless in a spa, all that movement and shooting jets of water would surely interfere with its effectiveness?

The other thing working at a public pool exposes you to is old people's genitalia. The water aerobics classes were a floating pit of flesh; breasts that usually resided around knees would appear on the surface to enjoy a few brief moments of zero gravity. I imagine underneath looked like one of those 3D ultrasounds: bulbous human shapes meshed together, impossible to discern if something's an arm or a leg. The wet perms and Tweed perfume mixed with chlorinated water made for a pungent aroma too. The ratio of the classes were roughly twenty to one in favour of the ladies. The men in the classes would be engulfed by a large group of senior females in their floral one-piece suits straining at every corner to contain their elderly flesh. They usually had a smile on their faces, those gents, and why wouldn't you? Secretly I felt that the instructor didn't push them nearly hard enough and I suspect many of them cheated and just pretended to do the actions underwater but let's face it, who would know and who would want to go and check?

There was one particular gentleman who would come in each day for the 8.15am water aerobics class and complete his morning laps afterwards. He did exactly four lengths of the fifty-metre pool, working at a rate of roughly three minutes per lap and he was religious about this, never missed a day. His name was Gerald, but he was referred to by the staff as Sackie. Why? Well, this lovely gentleman's testicles hung rather low, so low, in fact, they would peep out of the bottom of his swimming shorts. A hint of sack, if you will. On one particular morning, Sackie had on a pair of swimming trunks that were a little shorter than his usual affair, and instead of only seeing the tops of his plums we could see the entire branch. My supervisor had been fielding complaints from some of the mothers there for the early morning baby classes and something needed to be said. One of the lifeguards and I were taken aside and asked if either of us knew Sackie well enough to have that delicate conversation with him.

'Emy talks to him all the time.'

What the fuck?

'Shut up, Damien. I just say hello to him, you know, like any normal human would.'

'Emy, do you think you could mention it to him, don't hurt his feelings, just make him aware that he's exposing himself?'

'WHAT? NO!'

It wasn't like I'd be just casually letting him know that his tag was hanging out! This conversation required way more tact and finesse than I possessed at eighteen, and there was *no way* I was going to do it.

'I'll do it, I'll make an announcement over the PA.'

Oh Jesus.

'Shut up, Damien. UGH. Okay I'll do it. Just give me a minute.'

I was going to have to do it.

So now, barely a week into adulthood, I had to figure out how to explain to a kind, elderly gentlemen that his junk was on display for the whole of the leisure centre to see. All of the lifeguards and swim teachers were losing their minds in the staff break room as I left to do the deed – cackling like hyenas. Pack of arseholes, the lot of them. I decided to wait until Gerald had finished his laps and approach him when he was heading back to get changed. I felt sick. I didn't want to hurt his feelings and I really didn't want to be discussing his cock and balls either. I scanned the space and saw him lifting himself out of the lap pool. The moment had arrived. And so had his balls. I mean they were really slapping on his upper thigh, how could he not feel them?

'Hi, um, hey, Gerald. How was your swim?'

'Oh hello, Emy, good, thank you, I feel invigorated as usual.'

'Oh, that's great . . . Listen, Gerald, there's something I need to talk to you about. It's a little . . . ah . . . delicate though.'

'Really? Sounds intriguing. What is it?'

'Well, you see, I'm not sure if you're aware but . . . well . . . you're kind of . . . hanging out the bottom of your shorts there.' I pointed to his crotch and smiled in a way that I hoped said: 'Hey, no big deal, it's all cool, please don't be hurt by my words.'

He looked down and gasped. 'So I am! Oh dear, I'm sorry, Emy. I just rushed out of the house this morning and grabbed my old trunks and didn't even look in the mirror before leaving the change room. No need to at my age. I have diabetes which sometimes causes my [indicates balls with index finger] to go numb. I can't feel a thing.'

Diabetes! Of course! That made sense. He wasn't knowingly exposing himself, he had some form of scrotal paralysis.

'That's okay, Gerald, really, I knew it would be something like that. Maybe try different bathers? You could totally pull off a speedo and I bet the ladies in the aerobics class would love that.'

'Yes, yes! Good idea and I suppose they will support my area in a more sufficient manner. Thanks, Emy, I appreciate you letting me know.'

'No worries, Gerald, I'll see you tomorrow.'

I felt immense relief as I watched him walk away. I'd not upset him, in fact I'd done him a service! I noted he'd popped his towel around his waist as he strolled back to his locker and I went back in to face the lunatics in the staff room.

'What did he say? What did you say?'

'Shut up, Damien. His nuts are paralysed, he didn't know, okay? He's going to buy better bathers, just leave it alone now.'

'His nuts are *what*? Is that a war injury or something?'

'Yeah, Damien, it's a war injury. Hitler sent in teeny, tiny soldiers to bomb his balls. No, he has diabetes and that is one of the side effects.'

I never saw Gerald's ball sack again after that. Each day as he exited the change rooms he'd give me a thumbs up, I'd look at his dick and give him one back to indicate that he was all strapped up – it became our thing. What? Shut up, it was charming, trust me.

Besides unintentionally joining the mob, working at an unofficial sex shop and inspecting old people's crotches, another momentous event occurred after I finished high school. I lost my virginity! Yes, that's right, I didn't have sex until I was eighteen. I hung onto my purity for many years, held it close, waiting for the right man to come along, lay me down on a soft bed of roses above a mountain top while wild stallions galloped around us . . .

That's right, I wanted to lose my virginity in the middle of a scene from *Lord of the Rings*.

Side note: The phrase 'losing my virginity' has always seemed an absurd way of describing your first sexual encounter. Like you've simply misplaced your virtue in a moment of absentmindedness. The term alludes to the fact that you may one day find it again. Oh, here's my purity! It fell behind the couch. Fantastic, I'll just pop it back in.

I think it should be called something like 'irrevocable hymen removal' – it needs to be finite not full of hope.

The story of how I irrevocably removed my hymen is not the most glamorous one for someone who had clutched onto her virginity for the length of high school, not letting one single foreign object near her lady garden, while her friends were getting aggressively fingered from the time they were twelve. Okay, truth be told, no bastard wanted it; remember, I had the whole body hair situation going on, among other things. My first time was a little traumatic – I bet your first time was a let down too, huh? As it bloody should be! I'm so worried for my children. My expectations came from watching *The Wonder Years* and SBS world movies, but kids now are using horny teen sluts as reference material. Instead of just having the sex talk, which is now a walk in the park, we have to have the adult film talk. It's up to us to lower their sexpectations, explain that the first time they do sex it will be awkward, sticky and there may be some tears, that there will also be pubic hair and normal-sized tits.

The internet has made it so easy for our kids to come across porn, for us to come across porn. You can just be sitting at your laptop googling recipes for slow-cooked beef stroganoff and boom: PORN. You can't get away from it.

There is no easy way to have this conversation with your kids. How do you explain that some like to watch other people having sex? That some people get paid to have sex in front of other people who film them and then pop those films online for public consumption?

You'll be happy to know I answered this question in my 2014 stand-up show, *The Motherload*. I thought perhaps that if I put all the crucial information relating to pornography in a well-known children's song, it might make it easier for you all to explain it to your kids and for it to be digested by them.

'But, Em! I didn't see your show!' First off, wait – WHAT? You missed a pretty great time, don't let it happen again, okay? Don't worry though, I've thoughtfully included the lyrics below. Just make sure you hum it out loud to get the full effect. I did actions as well, but you can use your imagination for those.

To be sung to the tune of 'Do-Re-Mi' from *The Sound of Music*.

Em's Porn Song

Let's start at the very beginning
It's a very good place to start.

On the web there are things that you might see
Fake boobs, big cocks,
Pornography
(Pornography) (Pornography)

Virgin Territory

Redtube, Youporn and it's all for free
(Pornography) (Pornography)
Let's see if I can make it easy
Porn, a film, a film of sex,
Amateur, a film that's made for free,
Group, involves a lot of friends,
Showers, if you like a bit of pee,
Gay, a lot of boys on boys,
Anal, your sphincter could get torn,
Fetish, is sex with special toys,
These are different kinds of porn
(Porn, porn, porn)
Teen, if you want to go to jail,
Lesbians, prefer a muff to man,
Squirt, like a blowhole on a whale,
Spit roast, not a leg of lamb,
Midget, if you like the smaller folk,
Pregnant, a baby could be born,
Wife, let your mate give her a poke,
Just so many types of porn
(Porn, porn, porn)

Asian! If you like the Oriental look.
Shemale! Not a lady or a man.
Oral! When you put things your mouth.
Grannies! When you're turned on by your nan.
Public! Is doing it outside.
Fisting! Protection should be worn.

Rimming! A tongue in your backside.
These are all different kinds of porn
(Porn, porn, porn)

I'll let you have a little rest now. I'm also sorry for ruining *The Sound of Music* for you, or perhaps I improved it? If that's the case, you're welcome.

Back to me opening my frontsies swimsuit area to the public.

My V-plates fell off at my dear friend (to this day) Anna Deery's eighteenth birthday party. Anna and I have been pals since we were seven. We met competing in Little Athletics and later lived together just before I met my husband. In fact, she was an integral part of that happening. She was also an integral part of me murdering my virginity. Well done, Anna Deery! She chose to have her welcome to adulthood birthday at an Irish pub in the city. It was 1996, so as you can imagine I was wearing my best floral maxiskirt; a cropped tank top; a high, tight leather choker with a daisy charm on it – the pattern on my skirt was daises too. Fuck we were mad for them in the nineties, weren't we? I had a backpack purse on, of course, and my body had been drenched in CK One. I believe my shoe of choice was a platform loafer, which is an example of two words that have no business being near each other.

I walked into the pub feeling self-conscious about the hint of stomach I was showing in my cropped tank and looking for Anna, who was easy to find given the fact she had been six foot two since we were eleven. We were a funny pair, her and I, the short, loud-mouthed power wog and the tall, softly spoken Aussie. I spotted her and noticed that she was talking to a very handsome boy, a short power wog who wasn't me. He had shiny black hair, olive skin and green eyes. I needed him to be mine before the evening was out. Anna introduced us and I began relentlessly hanging shit on him as was my way of showing affection.

I had thirty-four Subzero limes under my belt when he made his big move. We pashed on the dance floor for roughly two hours, and I was completely happy with that, being the turbo virgin that I was. Then he suggested that we head outside for some fresh air, and I stupidly thought he meant we were going outside for some fresh air. No, friends, it turns out, he wanted to have THE SEX with me.

We began kissing again and then he suggested we lie down. I wasn't sure what he had in mind, though. We were standing on cobblestones in a small alleyway and the only flat surface I could see was a two by one metre skip close by. He felt the cobblestones were a good option and I was just so happy that this huge spunk wanted to be near me that I found myself agreeing, and so we lay down there. He then attempted to put his hand up my maxiskirt, which proved difficult as it was a maxiskirt with no leg split to speak of; whenever I wore it I had to shuffle like a mermaid to move around. We decided I should just probably take the whole thing off – makes sense right? So there I was, lying on cobblestones in an alleyway at the back of an Irish pub in my undies.

Not many pornos have that storyline, do they? He then fished a condom out of his wallet and took his jeans off – I remember this part vividly because after he'd taken them off he neatly folded them and gently placed them on top of the skip. Classy. The condom was popped on and THE SEX commenced and by that I mean he poked me a few times, I made some noises and then it was over. I couldn't believe that moment was the crescendo of years spent wandering aimlessly in teenage angst hell and it was nothing like I had imagined it to be. It was humiliating, it hurt and there had been a bin involved.

After we'd finished and put our bottom sections back into our pants, we went into the pub and held hands for a bit. I couldn't help but notice he seemed far less keen to stand and suck faces with me on the d-floor than he'd been pre-THE SEX.

Dad arrived at midnight to pick me up. Being a wog father, he of course assumed I would be kidnapped and taken advantage of if I were to get home any other way. He would drive any length of time to get me late at night. As I was leaving, I gave the man who took my purity my home phone number. He didn't ask for it, but I'd assumed he was too shy. This was a year before mobile phones were widely available; we still had to hover obsessively near a corded home phone, intercepting every call. If it wasn't who we were hoping for and another person in the house got on it, we would stand near said family member huffing, rolling our eyes and pointing to the clock on the wall.

I handed over my digits on a napkin and he promised to call me soon.

He didn't, so of course I became obsessed with finding a way to see him again. I truly thought that if we could be in each other's presence just once, he would fall madly in love with me and be my boyfriend forever. I'd done the complicated love percentage maths where you add the letters in your name to the letters in your crush's name and we got eighty-five per cent! You can't argue with those odds! I'd also read every *Dolly* horoscope I owned and managed to find at least two that promised Pisces some action in the romance department. The stars and maths were on our side, we were meant to be, I just had to find him first.

My obsession manifested itself into –

OH GOD –

I can't go on –

I just –

This is TERRIBLE –

We may never recover from this moment, you and I, so please try to suspend all judgement as you read how I tracked him down. Remember, this was pre-Facebook, Instagram and various other ways to safely stalk people from the comfort of your own home.

Are you ready?

My obsession led me to inviting myself to his father's funeral.

What the fuck, Em?

I am not proud of this but it's the truth.

Even as I type I am clutching my brow, violently shaking my head. What was I thinking? You see, I had taken to drilling Anna Deery about him on a daily basis: Had he mentioned me? Did he lose my number? Then about a month after her birthday, Anna found out that his father had been very unwell and told me as such.

'Yes! That's why he hasn't called me, Anna! It must be! His dad is unwell!'

Soon after that we found out that his father had passed away, and Anna rang and said that she was going to the funeral to which I replied, 'I'll come.'

'Emy, I'm not sure that is the best idea.'

'Nah, it'll be fine. I'll wear that tight black dress I just got from Dotty. It makes my tits look good.'

I know, what a heartless dickhead. My only excuse is that clearly my vagina was making all the big decisions in my life at that point. So I fronted up to his father's *huge* funeral – I'm not kidding, there would have been five hundred people. I spotted him and tried to make meaning-ful/sympathetic eye contact while simultaneously pushing out my boobs. With a look that hopefully said, 'Hey, I'm sorry for your loss, I'm here for you and I'm hot.'

Keep in mind that the last time he had seen or spoken to me I was lying on the ground at the foot of a bin and now here I was at his father's final goodbye. I must have seemed like a complete maniac to him – can you imagine being in his position? I had inserted myself into the position of 'caring girlfriend' at the funeral for the father of a man I had met for three hours one drunken night at an Irish pub. In my mind, though, I'd allowed him to see my vagina, therefore we had entered into an unspoken contract that stated we were going to be together forever. I sat and watched as his eldest brother delivered a tearful eulogy – I even had the balls to cry! *What the actual what, Em?* Of course they were very delicate tears as I didn't want to fuck up my carefully applied eyeliner, tinted moisturiser and lipgloss.

We left the church and headed to the burial, and I got myself in prime position just behind my man. I wanted to be the one he turned to when he was unable to go on. Can we all please remember that he had not yet seen me, at least I assumed he hadn't, as he hadn't come over and said hello. As they began lowering his father into the ground, my dude's mother, the wife, sprang up and tried to throw herself in the ground after the coffin! I was the closest one to her so I leapt up and grabbed her arm just as she was about to topple in. Her sons and daughters came rushing over to help and were also probably wondering who the teenage slut clutching their mother's arm was. That's when my man and I finally made eye contact. He looked momentarily puzzled, then it hit him who I was and then he looked even more confused. I imagine flashes of me, pants-less and lying on large blue stones were flashing before his eyes.

'I'm so sorry for your loss,' I whispered in a sexy, breath-less manner.

He nodded at me with a dazed look on his face, went to say something, thought better of it, and went after his mother and other siblings.

I was crushed at his second rejection – so crushed that I burst into tears on the spot. I found myself being comforted by large, well-meaning Italian women who thought I was upset by the death of my long lost relative and not shattered that the man I'd given my innocence to had ignored me yet again. Oh, don't worry, I took their hugs and kind words. I let those nonnas stroke my brow and feed me biscotti at the wake.

So there you have it, one of the most shameful episodes of my youth. Looking back, I honestly can't believe my behaviour but at the time it felt right and that is my only defence.

Did I ever hear from that boy again?

No. No, I did not.

Please make it stop now, let's turn the page and move on to the next phase.

Oh, that's right. It's when Em met The Gays and fell madly in love!

Prepare for all the glitter.

7
Gays of My Life

I'm a gay man trapped in a straight woman's body who looks like a lesbian – I cover all territories. And I've loved gay men from the moment I became aware of them.

In the late eighties my mother worked as a medical librarian at the Fairfield Infectious Diseases Hospital in Melbourne. At the time a great majority of the patients were gay men with HIV/AIDS. Some afternoons I would sit and chat to the patients in the hospice while waiting for Mum to finish work. I knew they were sick, I knew they preferred men romantically and I also knew that they were my kindred spirits. We would chat endlessly about Madonna and Disney and I was never once shooshed or admonished for being too over the top. My flamboyant nature was appreciated instead of tolerated.

The hospital is also where I met my best pal, Michael Lucas, who wrote that epic foreword at the beginning of this book. His mother worked as a nurse at Fairfield Hospital and we were thrown together at first, but quickly bonded and became firm friends. At the time, Michael didn't know he was gay. That realisation came much later, after we had spent fifteen years apart and he'd sought me out in Perth, in a subconscious move to allow me to gently assist him out of the closet. Once I left our high school, he and I lost touch. Just after I gave birth to Odette in 2007, he knocked on my door and it was like no time had passed. I was twenty-seven and about to fall off a cliff with post-natal depression and he was in the midst of a complete sexual breakdown, having just left his girlfriend as he'd realised that he preferred the company of men.

We found each other at exactly the right time and haven't left each other's side since. Rarely a day goes by that we don't speak. Michael Lucas is the type of friend that I desperately hope both my kids meet. He is the type of person who can succinctly and effortless write heart-wrenching prose, sagely advise on the darkest of problems and learn the entire 'Single Ladies' routine and perform it dressed as Beyoncé at his thirtieth birthday party. He is fiercely loyal, generous and smart, he never judges me, he is always there to provide a moral compass when required and has supported me every step of the way on whatever new adventure I have chosen to go on. We literally have no secrets, and I adore him with every cell in my body.

We affectionately refer to each other as 'bitch' and both take a keen, somewhat unhealthy interest in the state of Beyoncé and Jay Z's marriage. Our friendship reached new heights when we were able to see our mutual God Madonna perform live in Melbourne. We spent an offensive amount of money on the tickets, which entitled us to VIP lanyards, a program and access to the pre-concert function, which was full of other Madge tragics such as us. Our seats were so close we could see each fibre of her sinewy, muscular biceps as she dry humped her twenty-three-year-old backing dancers. We had also set about creating costumes that would hopefully set us above the rest; I think we were both secretly hoping to catch Madonna's eye and have her immediately invite us up on stage and ask us to join her family. I put more planning into this concert than I did my own wedding. Michael and his boyfriend Adrian dressed as backing dancers, which was a huge sacrifice for Michael, as it allowed me to dress as Madonna. He knew it was important that our overall look be perfect and therefore I would be slightly more believable as the female lead. He and Adrian made sexy matador outfits and I went as modern day Spanish hottie Madge. We were quite the trio.

We stayed in character the whole evening, and the only let down was that I couldn't perfect the crucial front tooth gap as my saliva kept eroding the black permanent marker

I'd coloured in between my teeth. Yes, I was willing to risk slight poisoning, such was my commitment to costume accuracy! Of course I have a picture to show you – go on, flip to the middle of the book. Look at us in all our glory!

My other life-partner in crime is a spectacular human by the name of Lyndon. I met him around the time my athletic career ended when I guess you could say I lacked any real purpose in life. I hadn't made it into the uni course I was hoping to study, therefore any need to be sober and alert had been removed. So I embraced going to night clubs with a ferocious vigour. I would head out on a Friday night and not return until Sunday afternoon. I had impressive stamina, in part due to the amount of ecstasy I was taking and the fact that runners, combat pants and tank tops were what we wore out in the late nineties. Seriously, every girl dressed like Sporty Spice – no one got sore feet and we had sensible slacks on with multiple pockets for the necessities. One night after some serious work on the d-floor at The Prince of Wales in St Kilda, I was told about an after-hours club called Freakazoid. It was a place where drag queens, midgets, gays, lesbians and everyone in between went to get their freak on. It started at 4am and went through until noon, and there was talk that an actual horse had gotten loose on the dance floor the previous week. I instantly wanted to go to there, it sounded like my kind of scene!

We should stop to remind ourselves that I was a nineteen-year-old girl from the outer suburbs of Melbourne who had only just started frequenting clubs and drinking. I dressed like a handsome military lesbian not the circus glamazons that were being described to me by a wide-eyed club goer as we were leaving The Prince. In all honesty, Freakazoid was the exact opposite of my scene but I was trying new things! I had taken good drugs! I wanted to see HORSES INSIDE! None of my pals wanted to come with me so I tagged along with the aforementioned wide-eyed club goer.

Right now if you suggested to me that I attend a club by myself at 4am where horses roam the room, I would cry and beg you to please not make me. Look, okay, maybe after a couple of wines I could be persuaded to pop on a leotard and swing by. In 1998 I was nineteen and busting out of the shelter that had been covering my life up until that point, and this place sounded like a dream come true – I couldn't get there fast enough. I arrived at the door of Freaka, which was chained off by some fierce door bitches dressed as sexy Muppets. I looked down the stairs into the club and that's when I saw him: a vision in denim boot-leg jeans; a leather-fringed belt worn at a jaunty angle; a ripped sleeveless muscle top that said 'Physical' on it; and a high, tight, white stone choker. (Note to reader: When I was writing this passage and called Lyndon to see if he could give me a vague idea as to what he may have been wearing out to a club in the nineties, he was able to recall the EXACT outfit he was wearing the night we met. He is the type of friend who will ring to make sure that our outfits will tonally complement each other when we go to events together.)

But as impressive as his ensemble was, it was the hair that drew me in: a breathtaking blond quiff, the most magnificent mane I had ever seen. It was truly lustrous, a masterpiece from every angle and when it caught the light, it sparkled from the shit-ton of glitter he'd adorned it with. Think David Bowie meets Bros meets Rod Stewart and you're about halfway to appreciating the head of hair Lyndon possessed.

Lyndon and I locked eyes and he came straight over to me and said, 'I LOVE that singlet, did you make it yourself? Not that you can tell. I made mine. You know if you parted your hair on the other side it would look thicker. Here let me.' Proceeds to re-do my hair, pulls out pocket mirror to show me his work.

Needless to say, I fell in love with Lyndon instantly; he was spectacular in every way. I couldn't believe that someone so magical was even talking to me.

After fixing my hair, he told the door staff (who were never going to let my underdressed arse in) that I was with him and we entered the magical wonderland that was Freakazoid. While I didn't see any wildlife in there – well, except for the leather queen bears – I saw pretty much everything else. The costuming alone! Of course, I never wore sneakers out from that night on. Lyndon and I would make our outfits together each Saturday after-noon in his little flat in St Kilda West. Hot glue guns, magic markers, K-mart kid's singlets – we used it all. That was eighteen years ago and he hasn't left my side since.

Lyndon has never referred to himself as gay, he is just Lyndon. Yes, of course he's a flaming homo, however he shuns labels of that nature. This entire book could have been dedicated to our friendship; he is loyal, trustworthy and would give me a kidney should I require one. We've not had one fight or cross word between us in eighteen years, can you believe it? I fight with everyone but not him, not ever, not even once. Lyndon is much older than he looks and yet has never had any sort of cosmetic surgery. Why? Let me tell you, he has not raised his eyebrows since 1995, such is his self-control. He often scolds me for frowning and smiling too aggressively: 'Emy, do you know why I have not one wrinkle? It's called self-control. I don't move anything from my nose up.'

I swear on all that I hold dear that he has staved off old age with sheer willpower.

Lyndon has some wild conspiracy theories, ones that would leave me wide open to litigation should I go anywhere near publishing them in this book. He values family above all and could build a house from scratch, furnish it and sell it without raising a sweat. In fact, he did just that recently!

Here are some of his words of wisdom:

- When you're angry always say things three times in your head before saying them out loud.
- Idle hands are the devil's workshop, Emy.

- Just buy the cheap coffee, you'll shit yourself thin.
- DON'T rub your lips or eyes, Emy! Dab them. Dab, dab, dab.
- My neck will never be wrinkly, I'll get a giant bulldog clip if need be. Grow my hair longer. You know I will.
- Put ice in your wine, then you're hydrating and dehydrating at the same time.

Lyndon also has an incredible depth to his character that only a few get to see. He has seen his family and me through some incredibly hard times. He is my general, there is no problem he can't overcome. When his mother was struck with cancer not once, but twice, he took over raising his younger twin brothers. When his father was unwell, he gave up his very successful fashion business to run the family one. When my husband and the girls and I needed somewhere to stay, he opened his immaculate doors and allowed us to live with him. He is a natural problem solver, a doer, the person I trust most in the world (besides Michael) with my worst and best thoughts.

Lyndon and Michael perfectly represent the two sides of my personality. I'd be completely and utterly lost without them. Truth be told, most of my close friends are gay men. I do have a few girlfriends who I treasure dearly who, now I think about it, all surround themselves with gay men too!

It may shock you to learn that I have only fallen in love with exactly one man whose sexuality was in question. I can honestly say that at the time it never occurred to me that perhaps the object of my affection wanted to be me and not in me. I was eighteen, and trying on a bikini in a surf shop when I heard a voice say, 'I hope you're going to come out here and give me a show.'

The voice was deep and I could see pair of tanned, immaculate feet standing at the change-room door. I peeked out to see a glorious Adonis with Jesus-style hair and biceps the size of my head staring back at me. My heart skipped several beats and I decided to take him up on his offer and go for a stroll in my bathers. I was still training at this point and had an impressive, athletic body. Sure my head was a little rough but I had body-ody-ody for days and I knew it.

'Girl, your arse looks like a peach in that thing. Have you seen the white James Bond–style bikini with the snake-skin belt? I feel like it was made for you.' He then went off to gather up the aforementioned Bond girl bathers and I was in love . . . Overwhelming, heart-stopping, vagina-tingling L.O.V.E.

We spent the whole summer together. Besides his rock-hard abs and perfectly symmetrical face he also had an encyclopaedic knowledge of all the Disney soundtracks and their songs, even the obscure ones like 'Just Around the Riverbed' from *Pocahontas*. He also knew the choreography from 'Thriller', 'Vogue' and 'Stop Right Now' by the Spice Girls. He was able to give me a French manicure with military precision and would hold me while reading Dolly Doctor, putting on a different voice for each letter. I don't know where you turned to pre-internet for loosely researched facts, celebrity gossip and yeast infection chat, but I turned to *Dolly* magazine. I could find out when a new can of Impulse was being released, who Leonardo DiCaprio was bonking and sometimes score a free Lip Smackers or mascara or a foundation that would turn my face an unnatural shade of orange. Who cared? It was FREE!

The letters in the Dolly Doctor section were supposedly written by anxious teenage girls, and if they were deemed too explicit for regular viewing they would be hidden away, sealed together only to be viewed by someone old enough to bust open the thin line of glue the *Dolly* people had popped in there. Needless to say, a sealed-section Dolly Doctor was cause for much excitement. As I type this I realise how ridiculous that security measure was – what was the point? Who do they think they were keeping out? It's the equivalent of having a porno ready to go on your laptop and hitting pause as your security measure. (Okay, that's the worst one . . . I promise, my analogies cannot go any further south.) I also have my doubts as to whether the letters were from legitimate teenagers. I now suspect the interns took it in turns making up disgusting and embarrassing medical conditions for fictional teens to fill the pages of Dolly Doctor. Either way, it was a highly entertaining read. It also delivered liberal amounts of glorious schadenfreude.

If you're not familiar with the Dolly Doctor section then I am sorry for you. I will provide you with an example below.

Dear Dolly Doctor,
My boobs are so weird, one is a B cup and one is an AA cup.
Do I have cancer?
Also, what should 'down there' smell like?
Help!
Candy.

This man was my soul mate. I was still a virgin at this point, I'd not really ever had a serious boyfriend and this guy's favourite song was 'Daughters of Triton' from *The Little Mermaid*. I know, you guys, I obviously needed to seduce him and make him mine forever.

He and I were to spend Friday night together, as we always did, watching trashy movies and doing each other's hair. I paid particular attention to my shaving and moisturising routine; I was like a greyhound preparing for a race – smooth, wind resistant – and I had matching underwear on. He didn't stand a chance.

He greeted me at the door wearing his mother's kaftan, and I noted that his legs looked particularly tanned. He said he was trying a new brand of body bronzer.

We took up our usual spots on the couch: me curled up in his lap while he expertly braided my hair.

I looked up at him and as we locked eyes, he said to me, 'If you had a gap in your teeth you could easily pass for Madonna circa "Borderline."'

To which I responded, 'Do you want to do it?'

'Do what?' he asked.

'You know . . . *It*,' I said and then I tried to kiss him.

He pulled away, shocked, and said, 'Emy, I'm GAY.'

Yes, I concede that perhaps the signs had been there all along in the form of Disney, bronzer, a Madonna obsession and his desire to wear his mother's clothing. Sure, he ticked every stereotypical box but I wasn't to know that! I just wanted him in my box! (You know I had to go there, it would be unprofessional of me not to.)

Things were never the same between us after that. Sure, we remained pals but the magic was gone. That same summer I did manage to find a human male to get semi naked with me; you can go back and relive that chapter if you so desire.

All credit to my parents, as I grew up in a household where the only thing people were judged on was if they dared to show up to our house bearing food. The ultimate insult as far as my father was concerned; how *dare* they suggest that perhaps the cupboard wouldn't be well stocked at all times and that an Italian feast could not be whipped up at a moment's notice! Other than that, if you were a decent human, kind to animals and loved music, you were welcomed into the Rusciano household with open arms. We didn't discuss people's sexuality, race or religion, they were just taken in and judged on their merit and sometimes which footy team they barracked for. Considering my mother was raised in country Victoria and my dad is from a staunch Catholic Italian family, the fact they both ended up such liberal egalitarians is quite astonishing.

When I met my husband he quickly realised that he would be sharing me with about five other blokes, ones who would meet needs he could never hope to; for example, discussing at length the merits of Madonna continuing on past her *Ray of Light* album or which Minogue sister you would save in a fire. So he accepted it and in time I think became extremely grateful for having the boys to share the load of, well, me.

8

A Fire in My Flexible Loins

Imet my husband Scott in late 1999. He was working at
the Victorian Institute of Sport where I trained a few
days a week. The second I met him I knew he was the one
for me. Look, I know everyone says that, but I really mean
it. One hot November afternoon I waltzed into the gym
and heard a husky male voice from the corridor. Images of
the Solo Man meets Russell Crowe circa *Gladiator* meets the
greatest fullback of all time, Hawthorn FC's Chris Langford,
instantly sprang to mind. Being a single nineteen-year-old
girl with limited sexual experience but desperately wanting
more, I hoped against hope that the person who owned
that voice had a physical exterior to match.

I was not disappointed.

A ruggedly handsome man greeted me – he had strong, meaty hands and a jaw for days. Is it strange that I noticed and was turned on by the muscularity of his hands? Honestly, it took me three seconds to decide that he and I were meant to be. I quickly discovered that his name was Scott and that he was a keen surfer, baseballer (explains the hands) and could do the splits three ways. Hello, ladies! Needless to say, it became my mission in life to make him mine. Now remember, this was still before social media existed so I had to engage full-body stalk mode for real. Kids these days are so lazy, they don't know how hard we had to work to learn the vital information required when you were keen on someone. There were no Facebook check-ins to monitor your crush's location, you had to actually go and get in your car and drive past their house to confirm where they were. I familiarised myself with his work roster and made sure I came in looking immaculate on those days. I mean I had my business IN CHECK, y'all. I would moisturise, shave and perfume before I arrived. Full-time matching underwear was implemented, I don't know why, maybe just in case my clothes fell off during a particularly intense chin-up. Scott also had a girlfriend when I first met him but that fact was only a minor challenge to me. My game plan was to pretend to care about their relationship and then to become a sympathetic ear when they started having the troubles I would be encouraging them to have.

A Fire in My Flexible Loins

They broke up three months after Scott and I met. Did I influence that? Well, the answer isn't not no . . .

Despite my very best efforts in ridding Scott of his girlfriend and presenting myself as Miss Universe every time I went to the gym, it still took him almost a full year to ask me out and the way it happened was so ridiculous, yet so him. We were in the weights room and Scott was giving my hamstrings a stretch, because of course he was. I was laying flat on my back with one leg in the air and he was kneeling over me pushing my other leg down with his body weight. Our groins were about as close as you could get with clothes on.

Lets go full Mills and Boon here so you can completely enjoy the moment my now husband finally asked me out:

As I lay on my back underneath the weight of Scott's rock-hard upper body, I felt all my senses heighten. Every opening my body possessed was on the brink of explosion. I was a spring bud ready to flower and all I needed to come of age was his pollen. Our bodies were so close I could smell his intoxicating manliness, it was a mixture of musk and Rexona Sport. I could see he wanted to ask me something, his eyes constantly searching for mine, but at the last minute he would look away, too overwhelmed with desire to be able to articulate his thoughts. All I could focus on was his knee and how tantalisingly close it was to my expectant, lycra-clad lady garden. Finally our eyes met, the planets aligned and he took a deep breath and said: 'Emy, you have really elastic muscles.'

WHAT THE ACTUAL FUCK? Disengage Mills-and-Boon mode. Disengage!

What does that even mean? Was it a compliment? What was the appropriate response here? 'Er, thanks?'

'I mean they really respond well to static stretching. I keep pushing and they keep giving. You're quite lucky.'

'Oh, do they? That's . . . I mean, yeah, I have always been flexible, that's never been a problem. I can get both legs over my head better than anyone I know!'

As you'll notice, I was desperately trying to steer the conversation back to sexy town. Hoping he would equate my flexibility with interesting sexual positions.

He didn't seem to notice.

'Being an athlete and naturally flexible is really great,' he continued.

Jesus, am I just going to have to draw this guy a map?

And then . . .

'So do you want to maybe go and get some food this weekend? With me?'

Yessssss! All my efforts had been worth it! I waited a full 2.5 seconds before responding: 'Yes, Scott, me and my elastic muscles would love to get some food with you.'

And so we did. We had our first kiss that night and, well, our first shag. Like I said, I knew he was the one for me. Plus we had walked the golden mile in the courtship stakes, one whole year of flirtation – my vagina was essentially Mount Vesuvius, ready to erupt with built-up angst. I'm only human, you guys.

The next day my cousin Jess sent me a fax (it was the late nineties) with a question mark on it, wanting to know the outcome of the date, and I drew a picture of a wedding dress and faxed it back.

Scott and I had been dating for four months and living together for seven days when I found out I was expecting our first child. It was Valentine's Day 2000. I know Scott probably thought he was going to get fucked that night, just not in the way that I did it!

I hadn't been feeling well for a few weeks but had put it down to moving and over-training – that's also how I explained the missing periods to myself. Plus I was on the Pill, so there was *no way* I could possibly get pregnant! It was my mother who suggested I could be up the spout. Even as I went to buy the test I didn't believe it could even be a possibility: I was twenty-one, carefree and, just to recap, *on the Pill*!

Peeing on the stick and seeing those two blue lines appear was a special kind of experience and by special, I mean terrifying. I sat on the toilet in the one-bedroom apartment we had been living in together for one week and stared at the pregnancy test in absolute shock. I had genuinely expected it to be negative. I was an elite athlete and in absolutely no state to be having a child. I was still a child myself!

My first instinct was to call Scott, but then I remembered that this wasn't just a parking fine or a fight with my best friend – this would drastically affect him too and what I needed was a reassuring pep talk not a panicked boyfriend. So I called my mum. She told me to get in the car and drive to her place. To this day I do not remember driving the fifteen minutes to my parents' house, I just ended up there somehow in one piece. Jenni was great about it – by the by, she's who you want in a crisis. Seriously, if aliens invade and are looking for our leader, send in Jen. The messes that woman has had to clean up for me. Mum told me that whatever I decided to do, she would support me. We both agreed it would be best not to tell my Italian Catholic father until I knew exactly what I was going to do myself. So I drove home and waited for Scott to arrive home from work.

When he walked through the door he was holding a bunch of roses (it was Valentine's Day, remember), so naturally I burst into tears. I sat him down and gave him the news. As you would expect, he was in complete and utter shock. He told me he felt we couldn't keep it, he said he wasn't ready, that *we* weren't ready, that it just couldn't be. Still in a daze, I agreed with him and so the next day I went to see my doctor and arrangements were made for the pregnancy to be terminated.

As I walked into the clinic on the day of the procedure I remember feeling like I had left my body altogether – it was as though I was watching myself. I sat down, was handed a clipboard and told to wait. For some reason, hearing my name called forced me to snap out of the fog I had been in and I instantly knew I didn't want to end my pregnancy. It was a moment of pure clarity. I have only had that happen to me two other times in my life: when I met Scott and when I quit my breakfast radio job in Perth. I handed the clipboard back and said, 'I don't want this, I've changed my mind, I'm going to leave.'

Thank all the gods that I did, for the result of that decision is one of the most glorious humans to ever walk the earth: my eldest child, Marchella.

Sorry, you guys, I've just got something in my eyes.

I wish to categorically state that while I didn't want to have an abortion, I support a woman's right to choose. All ladies should be in charge of their reproductive rights. I don't want any pro-lifers jumping on this story and making me their poster child. I am staunchly and proudly PRO-CHOICE.

On the way home from the clinic I decided it was probably a good time to make some tough life decisions, you know, since I was in such a strong place mentally, after deciding not to have an abortion and become a mother at twenty-one. The first genius thing I came up with was that I should immediately break up with Scott. Why should he have to carry the burden of my choice? I didn't want to force a child onto him and I certainly didn't want him staying with me out of obligation. I had the romantic notion that I would single mother the shit out of this situation. I planned to grow my hair out into a wild curly mess and wear it in a careless bun, held in place with the pen I would be using to write my memoirs. I would dress exclusively in corduroy overalls and white linen frocks, sometimes together, such would be my capacity for whimsy. I would definitely have a vegie patch and chickens and spend large amounts of time drinking tea in a rocking chair. So basically, I was going to join the cast of *Steel Magnolias* as the sassy Italian neighbour with the secret past and fatherless child.

Again I found myself nervously perched upon our tiny Ikea dining table waiting for Scott to get home from work to tell him that he was still becoming a father. He walked through the door holding some sorry-you-had-to-have-an-abortion flowers and I burst into tears again. In one long, snot-ridden sentence I broke it to him that I didn't go through with the abortion and that I was planning on doing it all on my own and that he needed to move out and move on. After five minutes of stunned, tense silence he carefully told me that he wasn't sure what he was going to do and that he needed some time to process the situation. Then he got some of his things and left. Jesus, fuck – that broke me. I mean, I didn't actually think he would leave! I didn't want to be *Steel Magnolias* Em! I didn't own any overalls, I drank coffee not tea and my hair wasn't even curly! I now know that he went to stay at his mother's to try to get some clarity, which I totally understand, but at the time I felt like he had completely abandoned me in an emotional desert, thirsty, barefoot and pregnant.

I still had one more mountain to climb and that was breaking the news to my darling father, Vincie, that his eldest daughter was pregnant to a man he had only met a handful of times. While he is a non-practicing Catholic, the guilt and primal laws are still ingrained in his DNA. My dad is progressive in some ways and traditional in others; me being preggo to an Aussie dude and not being his wife was going to push him somewhat. The day I told him I remember his face looking as though I had physically struck him. He seemed genuinely hurt and of course extremely worried as to how I was going to cope. He tried to be happy for me but I could tell how deeply upset he was. He didn't quite look me in the eye for months. It wasn't until he held Marchella for the first time that our relationship began to heal.

It was love at first sight for those two, so much so he gave Chella her middle name without consulting me! Luckily Marchella Vincenza is a pretty great name.

So I was twenty-one and eleven months, still an elite athlete and the only friends I had were gay men. Pregnancy was going to be a breeze, right? I would glow and skip and become Mother Earth incarnate.

Oh God, no.

9

Up the Spout

I'm just going to lay it down fast and loose for you right now: I hated being pregnant with the powerful heat of a thousand suns burning in the fiery depths of hell. Scott moved back in but, by his own admission, was not all that engaged with the pregnancy. I think deep down he felt as though he had been forced into this situation well before he was ready to be and I was the cause of that. He didn't attend the first scan and wasn't really interested in knowing the sex of our unborn child, so the beginning of my pregnancy was a very lonely time. Actually, lonely doesn't do it justice – it was a desperate, what-the-fuck-am-I-going-to-do? time. I felt like I had no-one to turn to who was excited about the pregnancy. I wasn't even sure if *I* was excited about the pregnancy.

Needless to say, at twenty-two I had absolutely no idea what I was doing. All of a sudden my rock-hard athletic body was stretching and pulling in ways I couldn't believe. You must understand, I was someone who had always been in control of the things my body did – I had been a high-level athlete and my body a finely tuned machine. I was a sleek, delicate puma weaving through life like a sleek delicate puma. You get it right? I was *sleek* and *delicate* and *cat-like*. Shove a baby in me and the puma became an uncordinated, bumpy hippo. I spent an offensive amount of money on a whole bunch of pregnancy books with floral covers, written by women who wore skivvies and front-pleat beige slacks, thinking they would show me the way. What I quickly realised is that most pregnancy books make you feel like a bad mother before you've even become one. I ended up doing a ceremonial burning of them all in the backyard when I was nine months pregnant, eating an entire wheel of soft cheese and sobbing as I watched them burn. The thing is, a lot of shit happens to your body when you're up the spout that no bastard tells you about. I always promised myself that if I was ever lucky enough to write a book I would include a pregnancy chapter in it, one that doesn't hold back, a proper field guide for bitches with bumps. I mean, obviously don't look to me for actual medical advice, I'm more about preparing you for the fact that you will never jump on a trampoline with confidence and without a small wet patch on your pants again.

Cross your legs, preggos, cos we be going deep.

First up, well done on getting yourself knocked up. You've got a baby in your guts and whether you planned it or not this thing is happening so onwards and outwards, eh?

The main adjustment for me was the transformation of my delicate, pink, rosebud nipples into large, fleshy brown coat hooks. Each week I would look on in horror as they spread across my growing breasts. By the end of the pregnancy I had a couple of muscular, fighter pilot thumbs ready to fly a plane at a moment's notice! The opening page of *What to Expect When You're Expecting* should just say, 'Bitch take a pic of your nips.' In fact, if you are reading this now and are still in possession of your original nipples get your phone out this instant and take a snap of your boobs.

I'll wait.

While we're waiting for the lucky bitches to take their nude photo let's pause to acknowledge the fact that most pregnant people will get bountiful bosoms during their pregnancies. This may be a good or bad thing depending on your resting cup size. As someone who had previously had pecs, I enjoyed being a whole C cup. Oh, but don't worry, I paid for that short-lived joy. Everyone talks about the excess breast situation but *no-one* tells you that after you're done with the breastfeeding your boobs end up flat and lifeless. That when you bend over they resemble a pair of tube socks with golf balls hanging down the bottom of them. Think about the tiny, useless hands that the Tyrannosaurus Rex had: ugly and disproportionate to the rest of him, getting in the way, hanging there like big fleshy warts. Yep, not many of us can escape the T-Rex tits. Lying down is no better, you get yourself a pair of pit tits for your trouble!

Welcome back to those of you who have just returned from taking a picture of your norgs. Shall we continue?

Let's have a chat about thrush! Fact: I basically had it for forty weeks. I really should have purchased stocks in Canesten, my whole downstairs area was a *CSI: Miami* yeast infection. The fridge was constantly stocked with natural yoghurt. I often wonder about the first lady to try that, the pioneering dame who had an itchy twat and thought to whack some Yogo on it to see what would happen. Then she had to tell someone about her discovery! That putting yoghurt on an inflamed lady garden does the trick. She is a real hero in my book.

Skin tags! I was covered in them. What good are they to anyone? Hateful little flappy bits of fleshy rice. They appear on areas of skin that are hot, *moist* or frequently rubbed, which sounds sexy but is the opposite of that. My legs were rubbing together like a pair of horny teenagers at a Blue Light Disco, so I had a dirty big line of skin tags running down my inner thigh.

Weight gain: So the books say you should aim for ten to twelve kilos. We've already established that 'the books' can go and eat a bag of dicks. Ever the overachiever, I had that covered after month number two. I was gaining weight like a prized heavyweight boxing champion, and the nurses would all gather to witness my weigh-in each month. I am ninety-nine per cent sure they were running an illegal betting ring on how much I would put on from month to month. When I hit the forty-kilo mark I begged my doctor to please stop weighing me. Yes, I put on forty kilos during my first pregnancy. Just so you understand how much weight that is, I was essentially carrying Tom Cruise.

Toilet stuff: Your body does this nifty thing of hanging onto your poo for longer so that it can draw all the nutrients out of it for you and the baby. This is inconvenient because *constipation*. I was straining so aggressively on the toilet that I not only got bum grapes (haemorrhoids) but I also acquired two burst blood vessels in each eye. I looked like I had been hitting a bucket bong pretty hard, which is such a bad look at thirty-five weeks pregnant.

Iron vag: For me Iron vag was the worst symptom of pregnancy, certainly the most painful. Towards the end of your run it feels as though some sick bastard has sewn bricks into your lady parts, they are so heavy – like iron. It feels as though all the blood in your body is exclusively living in your crotchal area, that at any moment the baby is going to pop out and say hello. While we're in this area you should probably just go ahead and buy undies in bulk, because the discharge is off its head. It's like your vag has a chesty cough and is just hacking up phlegm all day long.

The technical term for it is 'leucorrhoea', but let's just call it what it is: fucking gross.

So in summary:

1. Fighter pilot–thumb nipples
2. T-Rex tits/Pit tits
3. Mayor of Thrush Town
4. Skin rice
5. Bum grapes
6. Iron vag
7. Did you blow your nose in your undies?

How is everyone feeling? You probably want to set my book on fire now, don't you?

Let's go back now to the main event, the closing stages of my first pregnancy. By the time I was thirty-five weeks I'd completely had it, I'd given up on wearing clothes all together and would drape a fitted sheet over my shoulders should we have company. Scott had thankfully come around and was well on board for the arrival of our first daughter. How did he come around? Well, let's just say a *very* pregnant Em stood at the front door one afternoon and threw his clothes down from the balcony, telling him to get on or get out!

That vision must have shocked him into submission and I know I looked radiant (read: like a sweaty warthog) so how could he resist? At the time I felt immense relief that I wouldn't be going through the birth alone, but now?

As promised, the full glory of my *Australian Idol* head shot. I'm not sure what happened here. Someone needed to step away from the hair straightener.

Nana on her way to Buckingham Palace. That woman was a colour coordinating machine!

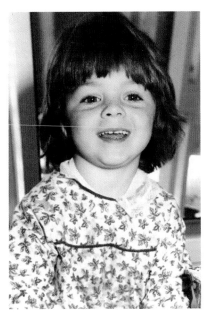

Me and my sister Abby rocking some of Mum's finest 'home haircuts'. Just a bowl and some nail scissors was all she needed.

Nonna and Vincie.

Mum and Dad.
Mum gave herself
haircuts too.

Above: Four generations of lunatics.
Luigi, Em, Chella and Vincie.

Left: Luigi and me.

My beloved cubby house before it was besmirched with Abby's name.

Proud, eventual owners of genuine Cabbage Patch Kids, Karen Larola and Celia Badelia.

Looking chic in the Doiymo school uniform. Note Diamond the cow's horns . . .

John Farnham's child bride should probably have his haircut, right?

On the podium at the state championships.

The crescendo of my awkward teen years.

With Dad and Scotty on my wedding day.

Fierce bitches. My glorious daughters Chella and Odie.

My boys, Lyndon and Michael, waiting in an alleyway for Madonna's secret show . . . because of course we were!

With Michael and Adrian at Madonna.

Me and Lyndon.

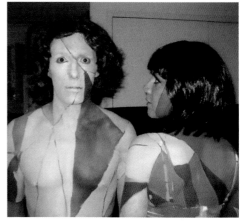

Me and Michael as Gotye and Kimbra, Halloween 2012. We take costuming very seriously.

I've come a long way from my first gig with Vincie AKA
the Em Rusciano band . . .

. . . To the sold out Palais Theatre
in Melbourne . . .

. . . And the Try Hard tour featuring the
very book that you're reading right now!

Just a stand-up comic, no fuss, no bells and whistles . . . That giant E was a NIGHTMARE to tour with. We set it on fire at the end of the tour.

Singing 'Somewhere Over the Rainbow' on my flower swing for Nana.

Look, I'd be lying if I said it still didn't come up in therapy. My abandonment issues run deep, y'all, real deep.

Around the time of the balcony yelling was when my baby's name finally came to me. How I came up with my eldest child's name is a story I don't tell often because it's a little bit ridiculous. I was almost nine months pregnant when the World Trade Center terror attacks happened. I vividly recall lying on the couch watching those horrific images and worrying about the kind of world I was bringing my child into. It became far too much for me to fathom so I flicked the channel and came across a show called *Beauty and the Beast*. Do you remember it? It was hosted by a sometimes unpleasant man called Stan Zemanek. He started telling a story of how his wife was becoming less tolerant of his ways and how she would watch the show and then berate him about his sexist attitudes when he returned home. I remember tearing up at this and thinking, *Good on you, Mrs Zemanek. You're a fucking SAINT for putting up with that sometimes horrible man!* Then Stan said her name, and it was Marcella. The emotion I felt about 9/11 mixed with the fact that I was thirty-five weeks pregnant made me sure that that was the kind of woman I wanted my kid to be. I wanted a woman who was strong enough to stand up to the likes of Stan Zemanek.

So in that instant I decided that my bump would be called Marcella.

Yes. My daughter is named after Stan Zemanek's wife.

I know. Ridiculous.

That being said, Marcella Zemanek is a fierce woman who tirelessly campaigns to raise funds and awareness for brain cancer and survived her own bout of the big C. I think she is fine namesake for my kid.

The night my waters finally broke I was actually sitting on the toilet! This is poignant as I had spent the entire pregnancy obsessing over it happening at a completely inappropriate time. I'd had visions of water whooshing out of me waterfall style, creating an amniotic fluid tsunami at Sportsgirl or Blockbuster, so to have it happen while sitting on a hole specifically designed for bodily waste was a bonus. I looked in and saw that it was *not* clear in colour as it should have been. It was bright green and I knew from one of the useless books I had sort of read that this meant that the baby had done a poo in utero and could be in distress. So Scotty and I jumped into our little Green Hyundai Excel and zoomed to the Mercy Women's Hospital in Melbourne.

By this stage I had started having contractions. If someone who has never given birth tries to explain contractions to you as a strong period cramp, punch them in the throat and ask them if it feels like a mosquito bite. Those fuckers hurt like motherfuckers.

Twelve hours of labour later and I had only dilated two centimetres. That is not much (I needed to be at twelve centimetres) for a very long time in labour for those of you not in the birth lingo know. The baby's heart rate had begun to drop with each contraction so the decision was made for me to have an emergency C-section. The anaesthetist was called in and I was told to sit still – while having contractions. Yes, of course, no worries, complete and utter piece of cake! The spinal block was successfully administered and I was whizzed into surgery. Quick as you like they yanked out Marchella Vincenza Rusciano-Barrow, all nine pounds of her and I was a bloody mum!

Then they took her away! I was wheeled into recovery and left to twiddle my thumbs, not having yet even smelled my newborn present. I cannot remember a longer hour in my life. I have since found out that Scott was wheeling her around the hospital showing her off to anyone who possessed eyes. Hadn't he come a long way? Never mind the person who actually did the birthing and was now a human ziplock bag. Finally, *finally* they wheeled me onto the ward and there she was asleep in a little plastic tub on wheels. I couldn't believe that little person was all mine, it was complete love at first sight. She was perfection. I mean it: my kid was an unusually attractive baby. All the nurses agreed and I could tell they weren't just humouring me. That first night was hell on a stick though. My milk had started to come in and my breasts had promptly gone and got themselves engorged. But she wasn't latching on and I was in a hot house of pain.

OH! OH! Let's quickly engage 'pregnancy guide' mode to bring you this special news report. Breastfeeding isn't a natural act that just happens easy as you like! For some it does, for others (me) your nipples end up looking like the baby has razor blades for teeth! Don't feel badly if you don't enjoy or can't breastfeed, that's A-OK. I persevered for about six months, and it did get easier, but I just couldn't really get the hang of it and she just always seemed hungry. So I started bottle feeding her and we were both much happier. A lot of well-meaning people will try to tell you that breast is best for as long as possible and, yes, scientifically speaking, breast milk is most excellent for your new baby, however if it's making your life absolutely miserable, then go the bottle.

Being a young mother wasn't easy – we essentially grew up together, my eldest and I. There were times we would lay in bed together all day, not sure what to do. I tried to join a local mothers' group in my area and as you can probably imagine, that was an unmitigated disaster. I feel the way they put those groups together is heavily flawed: 'Hey, you guys all just gave birth and live within a two-kilometre radius of each other, you've probably got nothing in common but why not get together once a week and talk about your most intimate fears and worries?' Million dollar idea: A dating app for new mothers. Think Tinder but fewer cock shots and more mothers swiping left or right on prospective mothers' group pals. Oh, your profile picture is of you and your Thermomix? NEXT! That puppy with you is very cute, I hope it's yours because I am hitting the YES button! I'm calling it Mumder.

Shot gun this idea should anyone try to steal it, remember you read it here first.

Chella and I have a different bond to my youngest and I. As though we went through a war together and lived to tell the tale. Marchella is fifteen now and is one of the most impressive humans to ever walk the planet. She regularly gets one hundred per cent on maths tests, is learning two languages, plays piano, is a state-ranked hurdler and plays netball at a high level too. She is level-headed, pragmatic and calm. If I wasn't actually present at her birth I would question if she was mine. I am so proud of her I could burst.

We're still great mates. Even if that changes when we move into the hard-core teen years, I've already had such a great run with her it doesn't matter. Recently I discovered that the name Marchella means 'young warrior', which, considering the person she has become, and throw in the fact she is a red-headed Scorpio, is incredibly apt. Having this glorious child was the making of me, although we do have a touch of Saffy-and-Edina-from-*Ab-Fab* vibe about us, but she knows I would throw down and go to war for her at a moment's notice. She also has an incredible relationship with her father, they are two peas in a pod. All those admirable attributes I mentioned above, she gets them from Scotty. I can really only claim the musical and athletic ability . . . and her need to question authority.

10

Strayan Idol

For someone who is a chronic over-sharer there is one thing I've never written about and that is my time as a contestant on the wildly popular second series of *Australian Idol*. *Idol* is the reason I am sitting here writing this book, I am under no illusions about that. *Idol* also set me on the path to self-awareness and self-reflection, it forced me to look at the way I behaved and the short comings I had emotionally. It was simultaneously soul destroying and life changing. I know – you wouldn't think a reality TV show capable of all of that, would you?

In 2004 I was living in Adelaide. Scott had been hired as a strength and conditioning coach at the Port Adelaide

Football Club and I was at home looking after our then two-year-old Marchella. I was also studying interior design part-time at uni, hanging out with a couple of the WAGS and generally having a pretty swish life. During one of Port Adelaide's games I was sitting in the bar at Alberton Oval with a few of the other wives. The TV was on in the background and an ad for *Australian Idol* auditions came on. For some reason it caught my eye. I had always fancied myself as a bit of a singer/performer. You recall my training at the Miss Sheila Fancypants School of Dance of course and the elaborate concerts I would put on for my family. I'd sung in public a couple of times, I'd won a singing competition at my high school when I was thirteen and performed in a Metallica cover band when I was fourteen – we only did one gig at the Year 9 social. I knew I could hold a tune and really nailed all the in-car power ballads I would belt out driving Marchella to and from daycare so I thought maybe, just maybe, I wanted to audition.

When Scott and I were driving home from the game I said to him, 'Do you think I should audition for *Australian Idol*? They're in town this weekend looking for contestants.'

To his credit he didn't skip a beat. 'Do you want to?'

'I don't know, maybe . . . I mean, I know I won't make it but it would be good to test myself. But . . . Well . . . Nah, it's okay. The last day is tomorrow, I'd have to get up at stupid o'clock and I'm tired.'

That was the last we spoke of it but I just couldn't shake it. I lay awake for most of the night thinking about what

I might sing and when the sun started coming up I woke Scott and asked, 'Should I go to the auditions?'

He looked at me through very sleepy eyes, smiled and said, 'Why not, you obviously want to, you've got nothing to lose, I say go for it.'

So I did.

On a brisk Sunday morning, I turned up to the Adelaide Showgrounds. When I got there I was surprised to see that there wasn't that much of a line. I walked up to the table that said 'Registrations', showed them my ID, filled out the forms, was given a sticker with a number written on it and sat down to wait.

I wasn't sitting for very long when a fabulous, short, ethnic gay man approached me. I later learned that he was Paul Riggio, the talent coordinator, and then much later learned that he'd made a very deliberate beeline for the Pink look-alike as soon as she'd walked in! He said he just *knew* that I had something to offer, that I set all his gay senses off and as we know the Gaytrix is a powerful force and rarely wrong.

Paul gently probed me and after a few key questions he realised he had hit the reality TV producer jackpot, AKA I had an impressive backstory.

Paul: 'How old are you?'

Em: 'Twenty-five.'

Paul: 'Married? Kids?'

Em: 'I have a daughter named Chella who is two and a partner, her dad, Scott.'

Paul: 'Do you have family in Adelaide?'

Em: 'No, I'm from Melbourne, they all live there.'

Paul: 'Where do you sing around town?'

Em: 'I don't, I've never sung in public before. I was in a band in high school and sang at a school assembly when I was thirteen by myself, but that's it.'

Paul: 'Okaaaaaay . . . So you're a young mum who has never sung in public and you're living away from your family?' (DING DING DING DING DING!)

Em: 'Yes, I guess I am.'

Paul: 'Can you please come with me. I'll take you straight in to meet Stephen and Greg, our executive producers.'

I'm going to take a guess and say that on that short walk to see the powerful men who controlled everything, Paul prayed to every god he knew that I could actually hold a tune. He had already ascertained that I was sassy from our camp banter session after the initial interrogation, and I didn't look like your average mother (shaved head, fauxhawk, tutu, combat boots, skull top, one earring . . . What can I say? I was going through my fairy punk phase) so he just had to get the final piece of the puzzle in place and he had perfect contestant Yahtzee! I was ushered into a small room where two men were sitting behind a table: Greg Burness and Stephen Tate. Immediately Greg started talking, he spoke fast and loose. Stephen was a little more measured and careful with his choice of words. They seemed a complementary team: slightly chatty cop/mysterious smiley cop, if you will. Greg had obviously been filled in by Paul about my backstory so he just started commanding that

I sing songs. I'm not kidding, I became a human jukebox as Greg would bark popular songs at me with a huge grin on his face. I knew every one of them and as I dutifully sang them back to him, he started bouncing up and down on his seat and clapping. He looked at Stephen and said, 'Let's send her to the judges.' Stephen slowly nodded and I was told to come back in the exact same clothes the very next day to sing in front of Marcia Hines, Ian 'Dicko' Dickson and Mark Holden. To say I was astonished would be an understatement of Herculean proportions – I still wasn't convinced I was being sent to the judges because I had any genuine talent; a small part of me was worried that I was one of those deluded souls who butchered every song their voice touched and when told that would respond with variations of 'But my mother told me I could sing.' Needless to say, I didn't sleep a wink that night. I also didn't have a babysitter so Marchella and I lobbed up to the final audition together!

Walking in to see Marcia, Dicko and Mark was fairly terrifying. The whole room looked like NASA mission control, a multi-limbed beast of camera operators, sound people, producers, make-up artists and cue card writers. Yep, those zingers Dicko and Mark would fire off were not always their own work. Greg Burness would come up with a lot of them and have them written on huge bits of cardboard to feed to the judges.

I took my spot on the X in front of the *Idol* sign and was asked to sing a few different songs. I think the one that made the cut was Christina Aguilera's 'Fighter' and that, ladies and gents, is when my story of 'lonely single mother battler' began. Even though I was not single, lonely or a battler that was the storyline I had been assigned and all editing was to be done with that in mind.

When Marcia spoke those words I couldn't believe it, I ran out to my support crew, which consisted of my two-year-old, Steph Wanganeen and Beck Schofield. Both of their husbands were playing for Port Adelaide at the time; if you're an AFL fan I don't need to explain who said husbands were and if you're not I'm guessing you don't give a shit!

The day arrived for me to leave my baby for the first time in her life and travel to Sydney for the next round of auditions. I was a complete mess on the flight and then I *made* a complete mess. My body has a fun quirk: high stress and anxiety makes my period appear out of nowhere. Surprise! Menstruation! I'm not talking a delicate first-day panty-liner oh-I-could-still-water ski situation either. The painters were in with such force that not even *The Block*'s Scotty Cam could fix it. I could have been a one-woman blood bank for a village in need. Moses himself could not have parted that red sea. I'm sorry if a few of you are uncomfortable about this and there is that thing about female comics talking about their periods, but this was no mere period it was VAGINAGEDDON.

I knew exactly what was going on and I also knew I didn't have any pads or tampons on me. I tried to assess the damage and by some miracle it hadn't stained the seat, it had been caught by the blanket I had around me. I stuffed the blanket into my bag, tied my jumper around my waist and waited until every single person was off the plane until I made my exit. What I didn't know was that there would be a *lot* of cameras there to document our arrival. Do you remember the scene where all the contestants run down the ramp at the airport because they are so excited to be in Sydney? Smiling, jumping, hands waving, full of hope and promise of what was to come?

If anyone has that footage, go back and look for the lone figure a hundred metres behind, crab walking her way down the ramp, hoping desperately not to be noticed. As soon as I saw the airport newsagency I dashed in to try to buy some pads and when I got to the register I realised that I had LEFT MY FUCKING WALLET IN ADELAIDE.

So let us recap, shall we?

I'm away from my child to do something I have never done before in front of TV cameras with a huge blood stain on the back of my pants in a different state with no money. Did I mention the fifty-seven cameras following my every move? Did I?

It was the clusterfuck to end all clusterfucks as I'm sure you can appreciate, so I did what I knew best and what I have done and continue to do every week of my life – I threw myself on the mercy of a gay man. I tracked down Paul Riggio and explained my situation. He lent me money from his own pocket and I was able to buy some fresh underwear and the appropriate maternity pads needed to stem the flow. My love for Paul still burns strong and true, he is one of the best humans alive. He is one of the reasons I made it through *Idol* with most of my sanity intact.

Most of the hopefuls were piled onto a bus but there were a handful of special people, AKA walking soundbites, that they put in Mazdas rigged up with cameras. Yes, naturally I was one of them. Feeling fresh and confident that I could sit without leaving a road-kill stain on the seat, I was able to relax a bit and take in the enormity of the situation. Here I was, a mother of one living in Adelaide just going about her normal business and then *bang* I'm going to be on the TV singing! Something I had only ever dreamed of! I had wanted to be a singer since the moment I could make noise from my mouth hole. However, Dad had been the musician and I went down the super sporty path. Did I know which way to hold a microphone? Did I know how to perform with a full band? Did I know how to arrange music? Did I know about pitch, tone and keys? Nope! Did that stop me or slow me down? Nope! As with most things in my life, I like to say yes first and shit my pants later, so when we arrived at the Seymour Centre the poo began to flow.

I am doing my best to give an accurate account of the events that unfolded during my time on *Australian Idol*, however please bear in mind it was twelve years ago now and I have blocked a lot of it out for psychological reasons. I believe, though, that what came after we had arrived at the Seymour Centre was the group rounds: we were given a list of songs to pick from and told to pick groups. I can't remember who I was with, I know they were all very good and I was the only non-professional singer among them. That would be the theme for my entire time on that show – a couple of the other finalists resented me for it, too. We sang Stevie Wonder's 'Signed, Sealed, Delivered' after having three hours' sleep and no food or water. It's almost like that's what the producers of *Australian Idol* had wanted: a large group of nervous, hungry, competitive performers in a confined space – who knows what compelling content might end up captured on film! Everyone from my group made it through to the solo line singing, you know the one: everyone lines up, sings for a bit, says why they should be the next *Australian Idol*, and then gets told to either step forwards or back? Somehow I was told to step forwards and found myself in the last round of solo singing.

We were down to the final fifty and I couldn't quite believe it. You need to appreciate how raw I was – I mean really, who did I think I was? My final audition was terrible, to say the least, my voice cracked on my last note, eliciting big laughs from my fellow competitors, and yet somehow I made it through to the final twenty-four and the live finals.

I suspect I was being carried by my big mouth and interesting backstory even then, and I remember feeling incredibly insecure about my spot in the show and feeling the resentment from the more seasoned singers around me that I was even there.

It was on that final day in Sydney that I made my first friend on the show, a person I still talk to now – the magnificent Ricki-Lee Coulter. Ricki had a big mouth, striped hair and her shoes matched her belt, scarf and eye shadow. She was a Gold Coast girl through and through and I loved her instantly, glad to have found a kindred spirit. Suddenly I didn't feel quite so frightened. Ricki was clearly one of the strongest singers in the final twenty-four and she had chosen me to hang out with so surely I wasn't all bad?

We had a head shot taken, oh my *Christ* can you even. Flick through to the photo section in the middle of the book . . .

What happened here? How did the gay mafia let this happen on their watch? I look like a recently electro-cuted cat! You can tell I barely know where I am: look at the dazed and confused look in my eyes. The angle of my mouth also says 'recently escaped from the insane asylum'. I just needed to dial everything back by a thousand.

We were all sworn to secrecy as to the identity of the top twenty-four before we were sent home and told to wait. I completely ignored the instructions and told anyone who happened to make eye contact with me that I had made the finals. I was to be in semifinal four, and Ricki-Lee was in that round too, thank goodness. So were future top twelve finalists Anthony Callea, Dan O'Connor, Marty Worrall and the eventual winner, Casey Donovan.

True to form I was terrible, I sang a song that didn't suit me at all and I looked angry for most of it. Not surprisingly the public were not into it and I was not voted through to the top twelve. Yet, like the slightly unhinged feline that I resemble in my head shot, I was given another life and invited back to compete in the wildcard round.

This time I chose a song that I actually like and I felt this was a bit of a turning point for me in the competition too. The song was 'If I Ain't Got You' by Alicia Keys and I sang it for Dad. Still the public weren't sold on me and I did not get through then either. It was only because of Marcia Hines that I found myself in the top twelve of *Australian Idol* 2004. She put me through as a judge's choice. God bless that powerful woman. So after surviving the Sydney rounds and then the live rounds with the multiple public rejections there I was, on national TV, doing what I had always dreamed of with no idea of how to do it!

So the *Australian Idol* Season 2 top twelve had been formed and we were a motley crew, let me tell you. Here is the team list, with a short description of each contestant to assist your memory, should you require it. I'll do it in order of mass public rejection.

12. Angie Narayan – Soul to her core, incredible voice, should have stayed much longer than she did.
11. Dan O'Connor – Tall, handsome, religious fellow.

10. Amali Ward – Young, smart, offensively attractive girl from Tasmania. Wore Ugg boots to her audition.
9. Emelia Rusciano – Mother of one who cried a lot and only wore one earring, looks like Pink.
8. Daniel Belle – Sneaker-wearing opera singer.
7. Ricki-Lee Coulter – Huge voice, big personality, Gold Coaster through and through. Ate a steak a day.
6. Marty Worrall – A bald head like Dr Evil but in possession of a heart of gold. Famously wore a white suit to sing 'Power of Love'. He's a good man, that Marty Worrall.
5. Chanel Cole – 'Quirky' and individual, sometimes compared to Björk.
4. Hayley Jensen – Golden-haired angel, a really sweet girl. I remember her being extremely driven and kind.
3. Courtney Murphy – The big boy 'fro! Court was easily the most musically gifted of our group. Wonderful singer and piano player.
2. Anthony Callea – Immaculate, compact, Italian boy with a big voice. At this point in time: straight.
1. Casey Donovan – Funny, brave and talented. Casey was only sixteen when she won.

We moved into the *Idol* mansion that sat on the banks of Sydney Harbour. Ricki-Lee, Amali and I had already formed a strong bond so we elected to room together. Casey chose to be by herself but was still just near the three of us in an alcove off our room. We had a man named Sam who cooked for us and acted as the mother hen of the idols. I still to this day wish I could have taken Sam home with me to run my life, he was one of the best things about the show.

To put it bluntly and to get it out of the way, our group didn't get along. More specifically, a few of us didn't get along and battle lines were drawn very early on. We were so dysfunctional a psychologist had to be called in to help us find our way. I now wonder if in fact that psychologist reported back to the producers on the tensions, as those of us who got along the worst kept finding ourselves in whacky situations together. A few of us took issue with a couple of the others, in hindsight, I now know those people were just 'playing the game' and crafting a public persona, but the raw, emotional loudmouths amongst us found it fake and it was infuriating. We were the same people off and on camera, others were more calculating about what they did and said.

The first week of the competition was upon us so of course, I got viral laryngitis. My voice box was empty, I had no sound coming out except for a strange guttural squeak. Seven days out from singing in public properly for the first time in my life in front of not just a few people, but millions and I had no voice to speak of. On top of all that I was already missing my daughter – I was aching for her. You must remember up until *Idol* we had never been separated for more than a few hours at a time. To make matters worse, she was in Adelaide and I was in Sydney, so I couldn't just nip out to give her a much needed cuddle. I couldn't even phone to speak to her. I honestly can't remember a time where I have felt more distressed than that opening week of *Idol*. Friday rolled around before the taping on Sunday and there was still no sign of my voice, so I was taken to St Vincent's Hospital to have a camera shoved down my throat to try to ascertain why my vocal chords had gone into revolt. I was given steroids and antibiotics and told to continue resting. I cried non stop. Luckily there were cameras at every turn, and a producer to ask things like 'Do you miss your daughter?' or 'Are you nervous about being on stage with no voice?' should my face accidentally find itself dry.

Our first live performance was upon us and I was yet to speak out loud. I was truly hoping for some kind of mouth miracle. Then, just before I walked out on stage, they played a video package, first up was my dad saying how proud he was of me (which is something I knew but had never really heard him say) and then my daughter appeared on screen. I hadn't seen her in two weeks – her hair had grown – and she said, 'Mummy!' when they showed her a picture of me. Tears were stinging my heavily made-up eyes and I felt a lump rising in the back of my broken throat, then the doors opened and I was on. My voice appeared in some form, it was a subpar performance in no danger of a showdown, however I'd managed to stay upright and not cry.

Not surprisingly, I found myself in the bottom two that week, and how I was not sent packing still remains a mystery to me. Angie Narayan went home and I knew that wasn't right. I had major survivor guilt and my insecurity at being in the competition went into overdrive.

Then I discovered a little thing called the fan forums. Holy shit, those places are where human decency and morals go to die. A cesspit of hatred and anger. I read the worst things I have ever thought about myself in my darkest moment on those forums. Thank *God* the internet was still only really in its infancy. There was no social media (OH MY GOD, THANK GOD TIMES INFINITY) only chat rooms where the depraved and horrible could gather to shit on those of us singing each week. No one was safe from the 'fan forums', so we all naturally developed a morbid curiosity with reading what was being written about us. Needless to say, several of us were sent into the depths of despair. So much so that it was decided to remove all computers from the house. I think the worst thing I read about myself was 'Emelia looks like a Barbie Doll that got her head caught in a blender, she should have her child taken away from her because she is so ugly.' I mean, that doesn't even make sense; one's appearance hardly seems like a valid reason to lose custody of one's child!

I knew I had to pull something truly magical out of my rear end to stay in the competition. It was then that I discovered that the fan forums weren't only frequented by those devoid of souls but were also home to some very kind people raving about the contestants they loved and voted for. I found one particular online group called 'The Lesbian Lounge' and quickly realised that they loved me best! You must understand that no one loved me best because I was the worst, but these ladies totally did! They had decided that I looked a lot like Pink (d'uh) and spent a great deal of time going into the songs they felt I should sing and the way I should style myself.

Needless to say I took copious amounts of notes and set about doing exactly as they suggested. As luck would have it the next week was 'Pop' week, so I picked Pink's song 'Family Portrait', had my hair cut a little shorter and wore the same dress she'd had on at an awards ceremony weeks earlier. I must admit I bloody nailed it that week – the song, the emotion behind it, the look – and it paid off. I received nothing but praise from the judges and the public got on board as well. For the first time in the competition I felt as though I had perhaps earned my spot in the top twelve.

I somehow managed to survive until week four, the now infamous Pauline Hanson week. The theme was disco and if I had been put on this earth to take part in one theme, disco was it. I went hard on the costuming, allowing the hair and make-up team to curl my short auburn (at the time) hair into an eighties feather mullet. I sang 'Turn the Beat Around' and then it happened. Dicko said I resembled Pauline Hanson on a night out at the bingo. I answered in the only way I knew how: I asked Dicko to 'Please explain.'

What I will add was that I had been at the AFL Grand Final the day before in Melbourne as Port Power (the team my husband worked for) had played and won. The next day was the Monday elimination show, and I felt sick all day. I had an inkling that I was going to go – I just knew. Sure enough I was sent packing that evening.

I vividly recall saying goodbye to everyone and sitting in the minibus waiting to be taken back to the house. I held my mobile phone in my hand, waiting for my husband to call. I waited and waited ... *nothing*. The entire country knew of my rejection and every family member available had phoned me except the one person I actually wanted to speak to. Where was he? Turns out he was very busy celebrating with the Port Power players! The 456 missed calls on his phone from every single person we knew didn't cause him any concern either!

I had exactly three hours sleep that night, then Stella and Jane, our publicists (who I also loved and adored) came to the house at 5am and I began my tour of the Australian media. I did every radio show in the country; I spoke for four hours straight. I was also flown to Melbourne to be on *Rove*, which I had been looking forward to since I found out I had made the top twelve, however when I arrived at the studios things were a tad awkward. I got the sense that Rove felt pressured into having the *Idol*

rejects each week and may have resented that a little. He wasn't very friendly towards me, which was upsetting at the time as I had long admired his presenting style and comedy. However, now having hosted my own shows and had people forced upon me due to network obligations, I totally understand his stand-offish reaction to me. I have since co-hosted his radio show with him and found him to be warm and delightful, which did take away the sting from two years ago and yes I am the pettiest person on the face of the planet.

Finally, *finally* it was time for me to head home to Adelaide to be reunited with my daughter and to get Scott's explanation as to why he had missed my elimination. The thing about reality TV is that once you've been sent packing, the country well and truly moves on. One minute you're being loved and adored by millions and the next you're back home in the suburbs of South Australia, soaking nappies and cleaning toilets. I must tell you, I was A-OK with that. I was just so pleased to be home, finally the ball of anxiety that had taken up residence in my stomach dissipated a little and I was able to eat solid food again. I had lost ten kilos in eight weeks and was a physical and emotional wreck.

I had only been home for forty-eight hours when my first job offer came in. Craig Bruce, who was the head of content at Southern Cross Austereo, had heard me interviewed on five different shows and thought I was a natural for radio. *Radio?* He first offered me fill-in spots on SAFM with the plan to move to something much bigger. Was that something I was interested in? Sure, why not! So I went into development with the biggest producer of radio in the country. If I thought *Idol* was a head fuck just wait until I got myself involved in breakfast radio!

11

Breakfast Radio and a Touch of PND

Well, here you are. You've reached the chapter I desperately tried to avoid writing. To be honest it just felt too big, too raw and too hard to be able to condense into a few thousand words all my thoughts and feelings about this time. Although that being said, I probably could have scratched it out in my blood, in a few words, on a rock, if pressed. Yes, you could say my time in breakfast radio damaged me somewhat. Nonetheless, I must concede that the story of how I became the hot disco mess you know and tolerate today wouldn't be complete without the almost five years I spent on air for Perth's 92.9 FM. Disclaimer: this chapter is a gentle skim of the facts with an in-depth analysis of how I was faring. I've decided to write it this way for my own sanity and also to save on legal fees. Just know it was tough, it was *really fucking tough* to take that route. I may still write the other version and have it set for release on the day of my death. Like Prince! Seriously, the rumours that he had a few albums ready to release upon his death have proven to be true. That is *so* him, he was so über like that. I wish I could be more like Prince was, be all about the art and not the accolades, but I'm so damn needy and desperate for validation. I would want to see what everyone thought of my albums, buy a brand-new crushed velvet tuxedo and be there to collect my Grammys and maybe sit near Beyoncé and Jay Z.

The other thing to point out is that radio was not something I had ever considered as a career. In the past, most announcers did their time on a small regional station.

Then, when they were deemed ready by the radio over-lords (forty-year-old white men in tight acid-wash Levis that cut directly up their nut sack), they were moved to one of the big metro stations. But I represented a new wave of on-air talent: someone who had a bit of a profile (AKA a reality-TV reject) but no broadcasting experience. This is still the lay of the land today. You have to be somewhat succinct and intelligent and able to tell a good story but you also need to be semi-well known. This saves radio stations having to spend money on telling people who you are through billboards and gossip columns. So if you're reading this and doing mid–dawns at Bumfuck FM hoping a program director will notice you and put you on a metro station: PLEASE STOP WASTING YOUR LIFE. That is not how this thing works anymore; quit your job immediately and start a podcast. Unless you're there building up your button-pushing and back-announcing skills, then carry on, it is excellent experience.

Okay, let's go back and take it deep. (Flashback harps play.)

After the *Idol* tour wrapped up and I had settled back into a somewhat normal existence in Adelaide, I started doing some fill-in spots on SAFM. I was lucky enough to work with all-round legend and wonderful guy Anthony 'Lehmo' Lehmann on his breakfast show a few times a month. Lehmo is one of the most generous performers I've ever had the pleasure of working with; he's generous with jokes and doesn't stomp all over you when you're on air. A true gentlemen among comics, I adore him still.

I was also working with a guy by the name of Sam Mac, who was developing his own radio show. The program director, Dave Cameron, thought we'd be a good on-air match so he asked Sam to have me on each week. He did and to this day, Sam is still one of my dearest pals. We have a very similar sense of humour and I am glad our relationship survived our time in radio together. At the time of writing, Sam is currently living with his four cats (count them ladies) in Sydney, he refers to himself as a SAMbassador of the Sydney Dogs and Cats Home (donate now!) and has an extensive collection of home-made slogan

T-shirts. I know, I can't believe he's still single either. He also recently became the *Sunrise* weather guy. So far this year he had bungee jumped, attended a rodeo and gone hot air ballooning. We initially bonded over our mutual love of eighties alien-themed sitcom *ALF*. He is a wonderful human, he makes me laugh every time we speak and leaves *killer* voice mails. One of the best things about writing a book is being able to tell the people you love that you love them and have it immortalised for all of time. Except if you get into a fight and then that shit is just THERE for all of time. I am willing to risk that with this guy. I love you, Shaun, don't ever change, best wishes and reach for the stars, your pal, Emma. (I call him Shaun and he calls me Emma. When we were on air, listeners would sometimes get our names wrong, so we started calling each other by those names. Look, we thought it was funny.)

So I was going about my business in Adelaide, doing the odd fill-in spot and trying to get back to a normal life after leaving *Australian Idol* when I got a second call from Craig Bruce. This wasn't about filling in, this was an invite to step up to the big leagues. Craig would later go on to be my mentor and mate, and I still speak to him regularly. At times over the years I have felt abandoned and let down by him but he was always honest with me and he was the first one to believe in whatever it was I had to offer and give it a crack. I have nothing but love for Craig. He was the talent scout and playmaker at Austereo (who own the station in your town that isn't Nova and has RnB Fridays), he made and crushed radio dreams. And he asked me if I would consider moving to headline a brand-new breakfast show. The strange thing about commercial radio in Australia is that you can often find yourself subconsciously wishing for the demise of another person's show. There are only a few spots up for grabs in the metro breakfast market so we all wait around like desperate crows hoping someone will drop dead so that we may pick at their carcass and wear them as a glorious skin suit. Other people must fail for you to move up the ranks. Turns out a show in Perth was taking its last gasps. I was in the car with Scotty at the time and we were driving to Melbourne to visit our families, so I told Craig I'd call him back.

'They're offering me a breakfast radio job in Perth,' I told Scott.

'What? With your experience? Fuck, they must really like you. What about your singing? Do you even want to do that? How early would you have to get up, you hate getting up early . . .'

'I think I want to do it, I mean it would be a huge change for us. You'd have Chella every morning, it would be full on. Also, would you be willing to leave Port Adelaide?'

'Yeah, I guess so . . . But seriously, how early would you have to wake up?'

'I DON'T KNOW, SCOTT!'

'See! SEE! We got up early this morning to leave and look how angry you are now.'

'Idiot.'

'Okay, so we're moving to Perth, are we?'

'I think so . . .'

How naive we were to think that the only consideration we had to make was how early I would have to rise each day. We didn't realise that I was, in fact, agreeing to be a part of a living, breathing beast that would take over our lives for the next five years.

So in December 2005, Scott, Marchella, Toby Dog and I arrived in Perth. I remember going into the studio in Subiaco. The old team were still on air – they hadn't yet been told things were winding up for them. I felt *super* gross about that. I had been hired first and had been told that my co-host was a guy named Michael 'Wippa' Wipfli (some of you may know him as he now does breakfast radio in Sydney). Our third team member was still being decided upon. Our program director was a guy named Shaun Gough, who was also new to the station; this was Shaun's first go at the top job so he was keen to impress. We began doing trial shows at night and chemistry tests until we settled upon a permanent team of Em, Wippa and a local Perth comedian named Ollie.

Now those of you who have been following me since *Idol* may notice that something happened to my name. Yep, change numero uno that breakfast radio made to my person was that 'Emelia' was considered too long and perhaps a little ethnic for the people of Perth. So I became 'Em', the fun-loving mum of one! We then had to have a session that would decide upon our 'roles' in the show, the characters we would play and the traits each person would have. We were told to not ever stray from the roles we were assigned. I'll never forget that day: a large sheet of butcher's paper was stuck up on my boss's door with my name written in black sharpie at the top. The following things were written underneath:

Em

1. Mum
2. Suburban
3. Local
4. Relatable
5. Female focussed
6. Everyone's mate

I wasn't a suburban mum (not that there is anything wrong with that, it's just not how I would describe myself) and I had so much more to offer than what was on that piece of butcher's paper. Why couldn't I just be me? Isn't that why they hired me in the first place? Turns out they wanted me to be *their version* of me. Don't think that didn't mess with my sense of self further down the track. I had super bad feelings after this session but I'd signed a contract and made my entire family move, so I thought I'd best push them away and get on with things. Here's another fun fact: I was also told that I was not to talk about sport, which I love – at the time I had an encyclopaedic knowledge of AFL as I had been listening to my husband bang on about it while he worked with Carlton and Port Adelaide. Apparently you guys don't like it when a lady knows too much about sport, did you know that? Yes, those words were actually said to me. If any topic fell outside of my role rules I was to play dumb – Wippa was to handle all things 'bloke'. Which suited him as he is about as male as men come. Ollie was a fish out of water from the get-go, that much was clear. He was an English man who had moved to Perth with his family and was highly intelligent and a bit left of centre. I think Ollie would be called a hipster in 2016 but in 2005 he was just called strange. I was a little too loud and brash for the gentle Ollie, though I was very fond of him.

When you first start out on a new radio show, every show has to be treated like a first date as you're courting a new audience. The poo and fart jokes must be kept to a minimum and the 'reset' technique is heavily employed. Every time we spoke about something in our personal lives we were trained to always 'reset' the facts around it, so it had context for first-time listeners. I couldn't just say, 'Marchella came home from school with a penis pen,' I had to *always* say, 'Marchella *my daughter* came home from school with a penis pen.' For a very long time people thought my husband's actual name was 'Scotty-my-partner'. The reset became second nature, and I found myself doing it in everyday life. When I introduced people I would unconsciously reset each of their lives for the other. A proud moment for me came two years in when my boss said, 'Em, you no longer have to refer to Scotty as your partner. Market research shows it now has traction.' Woo hoo!

Another thing I can tell you is that there is a checklist of stunts that seems to be mandatory if you take part in a breakfast radio show.

1. Drinking your own urine.
2. Setting yourself or your co-host on fire.
3. Drinking breast milk.
4. Jumping out of a plane/bungee jumping/abseiling.
5. Lie detectors (although Kyle Sandilands pretty much ended that for everyone).
6. Some sort of dangerous animal in studio.
7. Facing a phobia live on air.
8. Public nudity.
9. Listener wedding.
10. Piercing some part of your body.

Every time it was suggested that I do one of these (which usually coincided with a dip in the ratings) I would end up in a lengthy battle with the program director. I would always argue that it was lazy radio, that people could see through it and know we were just desperately trying to get publicity and ratings. I was worried we'd become 'Stunt FM'. It was a battle I seldom won. However, I am proud to say I *never* drank urine or breast milk on air – I have no comment on the rest of the list.

My first month on air ended with something I still talk about in therapy. I had been on air for a few weeks and was told that a LAB was to be held and that it would provide excellent feedback as to how I was being perceived by the people of my new home town. I later learned that LAB stands for Listener Advisory Board and that it consisted of ten people being fed free pizza in our studio with the mics turned on. I was sat in the producer's booth out of sight and forced to listen *to the absolute worst things I have ever thought about myself in my darkest moments come out of the mouths of complete strangers who knew nothing about me.* They were asked leading questions by the person conducting the LAB, questions to elicit negative responses so that I could hear them and apparently learn from them. Then they were given a Delta Goodrem CD pack and sent on their way. To say I was left reeling and reassessing my entire life on every level post-LAB would be putting it mildly.

Moving on.

What?

You want to know what they said, don't you?

FINE. In the interest of good storytelling and to avoid the wrath of my publisher Larissa, I will tell you some of the painful things that were said about me.

'The girl on the show sounds like a complete bitch.'

'Oh, is that what she looks like? I thought she would be pretty. She sounds pretty.'

'She is too opinionated. I don't care about what she thinks.'

'She thinks she is better than us.'

'Her voice is so annoying.'

'Her laugh makes me want to punch someone.'

'She's not funny but you can tell she thinks she is.'

'Imagine being her husband, poor soul.'

Look, it's not like I remembered everything word for word and am able to quote these opinions at a moment's notice. It's not like I went and recorded my laugh so that I could hear it and try to change it.

It was a horrible situation that I had not been prepared for, and I still struggle to understand the thinking behind putting me through it. My therapist suggests it was a way to control me, to put me back in my box, if you will. Why were the people of the LAB given so much power, you may be asking yourself. Why did my boss care so much? Well, in breakfast radio, the listener is king. You lot wield a vast amount of power, and presenters live and die by the ratings. One day an unassuming little media survey book may arrive at your house. Our careers hang on that book and the boxes you tick. Yep, it's trial by coupons. The ratings come out eight times a year and are taken very seriously by all concerned. In my opinion it's a fucking stupid, archaic and unfair way to judge a show. How many people under the age of seventy do you know who bother to fill in actual surveys? How they haven't come up with a different model is beyond me. The odds are stacked in the AM dial's favour as it's the older listeners who fill out the books. If this shit were decided on

Facebook the leaderboard would look way different, let me tell you.

I'd been in the job two months when my Nonna passed away. Violanté Rusciano was my dad's mum and the best damn cook known to man. She was also a complicated woman who had been through a hell of a lot when leaving her home country of Italy. The stories go that she once ran documents across the border in her stockings to assist an uprising attempt against Mussolini. It was casually brought up at the dinner table one night. I love those stories and hope they are true. And she deserved a medal for putting up with my Nonno Luigi! God love him, but you read the chapter on him, right? Imagine being his wife – poor darling. We flew home for the funeral and seeing Vincie so upset broke my heart. That was the first time I had ever seen him cry like that and it was extremely unsettling.

I wish I knew more about my grandmother. I intend to find out one day or try to get on one of those *Who Do You Think You Are?* shows on SBS so they can do the work for me. I suspect a lot of who I am comes from my Italian heritage. I know I look like her and I certainly have her temper.

It was only a few weeks after the funeral that I found out I was pregnant with my second child.

We had been seeing some real results in the ratings – despite what those ten hateful people had said in the LAB,

Perth was loving us! Me being pregnant was good in that it gave us a lovely story arc to follow but it also meant I would need to have time off when the child arrived. My bosses were none too pleased about that, and you best believe I had to say – on more than one occasion – 'No, I will *not* give birth live on air.' Our third co-host Ollie was also replaced with Tim Arnold. Poor Tim, he was mocked mercilessly by Wippa and I. He was an easy target, a bit nerdy and quiet. Deep down I thought he was very clever and knew that he brought some radio smarts to our egomaniacal team, however I suspect he was terrified of me and so he kept his distance. Tim was treated very badly by the radio station. We'd only been on air a little while when our new content director (we had four in my time there) decided to remove Tim's name from the show. He was still on it but didn't get a name call. I know, harsh.

Something else happened that year. After seven years together, Scotty decided to pop the question. I had given up on ever getting married; we'd already done the house and the kid so when he proposed in Kings Park on our seventh anniversary, I was honestly surprised. He had taken me out for a lovely lunch and then for dessert had set up a picnic on a hill that overlooked the Swan River. He had been quiet for a few minutes, which was odd, and then he turned to me, lifted my sunnies off my nose and asked, 'Emy, would you like to marry me?'

I looked at him stunned, genuinely stunned, and then remembered that he needed an answer!

175

'Really? Ha! Yes, yes, I would!' I replied.

So just to reset: I was still dealing with the death of my grandmother, I had a four-year-old, I was pregnant, I was planning a wedding, I had just bought a house and I was doing breakfast radio. What could go wrong?

I literally worked until the day I gave birth. I got off air and went to Sir Charles Gairdner Hospital and had my baby, a little girl – well, she was almost ten pounds, so 'little' is pushing it. My glorious youngest child, Odette Violanté, came into my life. When I look at her I often thank the stars that she has no recollection of her first year of life – if she did I suspect she would cry every time I came near her.

I knew about a month in that something wasn't right. I was having trouble bonding with Odette. I didn't feel the euphoria I had with my first child, Marchella, and some-times it felt as though I'd been given someone else's child. Odette was an excellent baby, she never cried, slept all night from very early on and was a good eater.

I returned to work six weeks after I gave birth and, looking back, that was mistake number one. I was still breastfeeding and trying to do breakfast radio hours; what kind of lunatic does that to themselves? The type of lunatic who is looking for a distraction from how shit she is feeling, that's who. I couldn't find happiness in the usual places, everything was an effort and I was tired all the time but couldn't sleep. The overwhelming feeling though was guilt: all-consuming, breathtaking guilt. Who was I to be feeling unhappy? How *dare* I? Each morning I would wake up and say to myself, 'Get your shit together, Rusciano,' but I just couldn't. I became proficient at pretending everything was okay for three hours on air each morning but as soon as the mics were off it was a different story altogether.

Then one morning I couldn't pretend any more. Odette was eight months old and I felt completely broken on the inside. I remember lying with her beside me in bed. Scotty was with us, and I looked over at him and blurted out, 'I just can't do it today, Scotty.'

'What's that, Emy?'

'Life,' I replied.

He looked over at me and I think realised this was above my normal complaining, possibly because I was completely devoid of emotion when I said it. Normally I would scream at him in a rush of anger or tears, but this time was different: I was disconnected and almost numb. I knew he was worried. He went into Mr Fix-it mode and made me make an appointment with my doctor. Perhaps I just needed to get my iron levels tested and maybe get something to help me sleep. I scraped myself out of bed and put on my best pair of tracksuit pants (another alarming sign, I never wore those things in public) and Scotty drove me to the doctor. I walked in feeling shattered and a failure. I felt like saying out loud that I wasn't coping with living. It was as though telling Scotty how I felt had opened the floodgates and given my brain permission to believe what I had long been trying to push aside.

My name was called and I found myself in a small examination room explaining how I was having trouble sleeping, how I felt sad, angry and irritable all the time, that I was having trouble eating, that my thoughts were almost exclusively negative and how the guilt, oh the guilt, was unbearable.

My doctor put her hand on my shoulder and said, 'Em, I suspect you have post-natal depression.'

Whoa there, lady. *What did you just say?*

'What? No, I don't.' Of course, I knew more than the person who had been to medical school and done extensive training in the area, so I was an expert.

'Yes, you do, and we need to get you in for some treatment immediately.'

What did she mean 'treatment'? Did it require a straitjacket and padded cell? What did she mean by 'imme-diately'? Was I so bad that it couldn't wait another second to be addressed?

She assured me that it did not involve anything of that nature and put me on a mental health plan. I walked out in a daze, part relieved that there was a reason I had turned into a sad turbo bitch, and part horrified that I didn't pick it up myself. Then the panic hit, and I was convinced that they'd take my kids away from me. I thought I would probably lose my job and everyone would think I was nuts. As you can see, I was in a totally rational frame of mind. The most terrifying part was trying to keep this a secret from the people I worked with, but then

I decided I was far too exhausted to pretend anymore, so I phoned my boss and explained that I would like to make an announcement on air the very next day. We'd built up a certain amount of trust, my boss and I, so he gave the go ahead. I didn't tell Wippa or Tim what I was going to say either. I knew that if I even mentioned the word depression I would be met with resistance. To be honest, I truly feared a backlash – who was I to be feeling this way? I had a great job, a husband who loved me and two beautiful kids. But live on air at 8.05am the very next day after being told I had it, I announced to Perth that I had post-natal depression, I carefully detailed what I had been going through, listed the symptoms and confessed my fears as to what would happen next.

Then there was silence as my two co-hosts took in the information. For once Wippa was lost for words, but Tim was a true professional and threw to the phones, which had started going into meltdown. Instead of the ridicule and skepticism I had been worried about, love came. So much love and support came at me I didn't know what to do. The other thing that happened as a result was other women recognising the signs in themselves and being inspired to seek help. We also had husbands, dads, mums, brothers and sisters recognising the symptoms in someone they loved. It was truly amazing and one of the best moments I'd ever had in radio – even, I guess, in my life. Any selfish fears I'd had about making this admission on air were wiped out with the knowledge that I'd been able to help other women who were dealing with similar feelings to me.

So I started seeing a psychiatrist, a counsellor, a personal trainer and a reiki master. I went on a full attack! That's the only way I know how to deal. I was admitted into a private facility for a couple of days during a ratings break. Yes, I had to wait until a break in the ratings season to be admitted to a psychiatric hospital.

My recovery was a very slow process. I had good days and I had really terrible ones. I did do a lot of cognitive behaviour therapy, which helped. And by the time Odette tuned two, I was pretty much back to normal – well, my version of that, at least.

The great news is, Odette is now nine and it hasn't affected our relationship in the slightest. I had a deep-seated, gnawing fear that my depression would affect her and me for all of time. It really hasn't had an impact at all, she is so delicious and loving that it is sometimes over-whelms me in the best possible way.

So this is the part where I tell you that support is available and it's important to seek help early – the sooner the better. With the right treatment, most people recover.

If you think you may be depressed or have an anxiety condition, or you know someone who might, talk about it and seek help from your doctor.

I am a very proud beyondblue ambassador.

On 1 of September 2007 my day of days arrived. I was getting married!

Instead of me telling you about the glorious day that it was, I thought perhaps you may enjoy hearing about it from my Nana's perspective. My wonderful Grandmother Denise, who is no longer with us and who you will read about later, sent me an eloquently handwritten blow-by-blow account of the day. It came in an envelope that said:

'Emelia – just thought you may like to read and perhaps keep for posterity my thoughts on your wedding. Nana N'

And her account went like this:

Scott and Emelia's Wedding.

Much planning and preparation was put into this wedding – lots of phone calls I imagine between Jenni and Emelia. [Em: Truth be told my mother did the lion's share of organising back in Melbourne, as I was very busy slowly losing my mind over in Perth.]

Jenni left no stone unturned to make it into a lovely and memorable occasion. Jenni consulted different experienced 'wedding planners' beforehand and drew up quite an exten-sive list of 'things to do'! Emelia has lists, too, I am told and would ring Jenni at odd times with suggestions and problems. [Em: CLASSIC NANA! All the subtlety of a velvet sledge-hammer. In the lead-up I would sometimes ring Mum in the middle of the night with ridiculous worries, she was bang on the money there.] *'Susie' I think was actually 'the town planner' and with her eventually it all fell into place.*

[Em: Indeed she was! Susie is an interior designer I worked for just after Marchella was born. She worked closely with Mum on the styling of the day. I had told them I wanted an enchanted forest and that fresh flowers were to be the only things used as decoration. Okay Em, CALM DOWN.]

The trees were a worry and at the finish of the time for their budding – but they cooperated and actually budded or 'leaft'. [Em: I told you I demanded a forest. Mum sourced miniature cherry trees that were due to bloom around the time of the wedding. In the lead-up Mum and Dad had twenty of them in their lounge room and ran the heaters day and night to encourage the blossoming of the tiny delicate pink buds! I think they're still paying off their heating bill from September 2007! I know, I was totally OUT OF CONTROL.] *They were set out in groups in the reception area and looked fine. Masses and masses of flowers in vases gave off a lovely perfume and were a riot of colour.*

I was told that 200 bunches had been purchased at the flower market earlier in the morning – tulips and lilies and roses stood out. [Em: She's right, Susie and Mum set out *very* early in the morning the day before the wedding and pretty much emptied out the flower markets to acquire my flowers.]

The guests waited sitting in white chairs by the lake side – Mother duck and her eight babies waddled by and slid silently into the water. [Em: God, I miss her so much. This sentence betrays her past as a kindergarten teacher. When I was little, she'd come down to visit us and we'd go on walks together. She'd always notice the animals, and give them personalities and names. She would also tell me about the goings-on with her chickens and the birds that visited her each day. She had the most wonderful imagination.]

Quite a length of white carpet runner was in place and a quiet break in the guests' chatter made us aware that the bride and her dad were on the way. A smiling Scott was waiting expectantly with the wedding celebrant – string music played quietly to the side.

All eyes turned to watch Emelia's entrance but it was a dainty little girl with a Red Riding Hood basket bobbing up and down, putting not scattering rose petals along the carpet. The look of concentration on her face was worth seeing. [Em: Marchella did indeed approach the rose petal duties with fierce determination.]

The lady celebrant was charming and polished with her wedding ceremony. Emelia and Scott's own promises were well thought out so hopefully they will be long standing. Photos were taken nearer the actual Ripponlea building, lots by family members and by the professional photographer. Just as the sun was setting we the guests moved to the veranda by the pool for drinks and nibbles. Through the windows could be seen the layout of the tables and chairs and masses of flowers, quite a spectacular sight. The main course of tender steak and greens on a bed of sweet potatoes was eaten by all in a short time.

The dessert – well different but again enjoyable. There must have been six, seven or maybe eight varieties being served

thoughout the evening. The soufflés in miniature coffee mugs,
no really doll tea-set size cup and saucers, were really different
I thought. I had two intact and I know of a guest who had four.
Really yummy!

The music was lovely to listen to and to sit and watch the
would be dancers was a pleasure to me. The evening closed all
too soon with Emelia and Vince singing a duet.

So there you have it, I don't think I could have described it
better than that. Big ups to Jenni and Vince for forking out
a small fortune on my wedding. Mum managed to secure
the venue I had wanted since I was a little kid. She made
flowers and trees bud on command and both of my daughters behaved like little legends on the day. It was all fairly
magical, it really was.

Scott and I didn't go on a honeymoon as I had to get
back on air. I didn't realise it at the time but Wippa was
planning his escape from Perth and I'm sure if you asked
him, from me too. He landed a gig on Nova in Sydney and
quietly left Perth and it was left up to our boss to call
and tell me. I was shocked to tell you the truth, we'd had
three years on air together, he'd MC'd my wedding and
basically been at the birth of my child and not a word
was said. I guess that gives you some indication as to the
state of our relationship at that point.

We were both at fault for the most part, and I am sure he feels traumatised about his time working with me. I was, at times, the very worst version of myself. My old pal Sam Mac came on board to replace Wippa and we had a much easier time together. But the hours were starting to take a toll on me as was my depression and I was becoming a very unpleasant person to be around. It's a wonder Sam still talks to me. He and I also became increasingly frustrated with the formulaic shows being churned out, the way we had to treat our listeners as though they were children and the parade of inexperienced producers that were sent to us to learn how to do their job before heading to the big leagues: Sydney or Melbourne.

Would you like to know the incident that caused me to storm out of 92.9FM in a blaze of glory? Of course you do, and if you don't, just skip right ahead to the next chapter. Teaser: It involves me being called about the worst thing you can call a woman by my boss in front of one hundred staff members. What a hook! I bet you'll all hang around until after the break to see what happened.

The most challenging thing we did on air were 'rescues': the station would help out a family/individual who was going through a tough time. We didn't always get these right, and many questioned their place in the show entirely. You would've heard these: the host's tone changes and the emotive music begins to play in the background (think REM's 'Everybody Hurts'), then a guest is welcomed on air to tell their sad story and we 'rescue' them with cash and prizes.

Oh my God, I am cringing even now just thinking about what I am going to tell you. *Holy shit*, this is bad. Prepare yourselves.

The day I quit my job we'd had one particularly upsetting rescue: a lady who had come on to say that her mother had terminal cancer and was not long for this Earth. She explained that she just wanted to do something nice for her mum, however money had been tight due to all the treatment and medication she needed. I had *stupidly* not read the prize sheet before we went to air – normally I did to make sure the prize was appropriate, however on that day I had neglected to do so. As I was speaking the words on air I immediately wished I could have sucked them back in. We gave the lady with terminal cancer tickets to see Christina Aguilera, a ride in a Hummerzine and a dinner at a pub.

All with thanks to Innovative Hair Loss Solutions.

Can it get worse?

Of course it can.

When the segment finished and she was *still on hold*, we played a song by T.I. called 'Dead and Gone'.

Recap:

- We gave her Christina Aguilera tickets and a chicken parma – as compensation for dying.
- We had a hair loss company as the sponsor – she'd lost all her hair from having chemo.
- We then played a song called 'Dead and Gone' – while the terminally ill lady's daughter was on hold.

We'd achieved the holy trinity of clusterfucks.

Once the show was over, I stormed out of the studio and started ripping our producer a new anus. I SAVAGED him. I was mortified, and I wanted blood. Then my boss called me in and told me to calm down.

RED RAG MEET BULL.

I went outside to get some air and managed to collect my thoughts. When I came back in my boss said to me, 'Em, we need the Twitter password. Innovative Hair Loss Solutions need another plug. They're not happy with how that segment went on air.'

Oh really? Yeah, I get that, I know how they feel!

I ran our show's Twitter account. I had built it up to thousands of followers and fiercely protected the account from advertisers and radio spam.

'No. I will not give you the password.' I was resolute. No-one would ever protect a piece of information more fiercely than I did at that point in time. I was prepared to go to the end on this one. There was absolutely no way I was giving up that password. I felt out of control and that was the one thing I could control.

'Em, give me the password now.'

'No. I will not.'

'Em!'

'No. Stop asking me, I *will not* give you the password. *Ever.*' Think about that scene in *Braveheart* where they are disembowelling William Wallace AKA Mel Gibson and he is banging on about his freedom – that was me.

'Em, I'm so tired of this shit.' (Note to reader: the lawyers have made me take out what happened next, but let's just say it was enough for me to quit my job.) After he said the thing, everyone in our open-plan office stopped making whatever noise they had been making and turned to look at me.

To be honest, I *could* be a bit of the thing that he called me. I accept that, but hearing it said out loud was jarring and it broke me. I was an enigma at that station. I know people feared me, I know a lot of people thought I was aloof and a diva because I didn't engage with them or hang out with them on the weekends. I bet quite a few of them wanted to high five my boss after he said that most terrible thing to me, but I wanted to throw up. I thought to myself, *FUCK YOU, mate. After everything I have given up for this job, coming back to work six weeks after giving birth with my C-section scar still fresh, working through depression, living my wedding and birth of my daughter out on air, early mornings and late nights, you don't get to say that to me.*

So I marched myself up to my general manager's office and resigned.

Just like that.

Four years on air dealing with deaths, births, marriages and depression all ended in five minutes.

When I was driving home I suddenly realised that we were going to be in a world of hurt financially. I had obviously not discussed this course of action with my husband, and we had a mortgage, cars and school fees to pay and I was the primary earner. When I told Scott what I'd done he was happy – it turns out he wasn't too fond of the person

I had become either. So we packed up, sold up, got rid of our cars and moved home to Melbourne.

And in with my parents.

Before we move on, I'd like to acknowledge a few people who kept me going when I was at the very brink of breaking into a thousand pieces. Dr Travis Kemp, who still looks after my head, was integral in my recovery. Dean Roepen, my rescuer on so many occasions, your friendship and tolerance of my erratic and outrageous behaviour shall never be forgotten. Louise and Ian Whittaker, our English pals who were also away from their family and friends – you became our family and generously took care of my children when I could not. Finally to Lara Kov, you never judged me, you allowed me to be the best and worst versions of myself. We are fierce bitches to the end.

12

Starting Over

Arriving home to Melbourne after five years away – years that included being on *Australian Idol*, radio/TV and much career success – with no job and nowhere to live was a fairly sobering experience. I was not returning a triumphant hero, I was returning a broken-down reality-TV contestant who had quit her high-paying radio job for no good reason and put her family into financial hardship without consulting them first. We went to stay with my parents and set about desperately trying to find somewhere to rent, which proved quite difficult given the fact that both Scott and I were unemployed and had no recent rental history, as we had owned our house in Perth.

We'd been back a week when an incident at my mother's dry cleaners took place. I'd found a stash of my 'good clothes' that had just been shoved unwashed into a bag, such was my head space at the time of packing – leaving Perth had been a ram-shit-into-boxes-and-run type of move. But I knew that Mum swore by her dry cleaners so I asked her what their address was and if they were expensive. She eyed me suspiciously, as though she was sizing up if I was worthy of using her beloved house of clean. Clearly, she felt I was not.

Em: 'Mum, what's the address of your dry cleaners?'

Mum: 'Why? Can't you wash them yourself? You don't exactly have a job.'

Em: 'MUM!'

Mum: 'Fine, okay, they're just near the dodgy massage place, near the ATM.'

Em: 'Thank you.'

My mother had an unhealthy obsession with the dodgy massage parlour with its tinted windows, neon 'Open 24hrs' sign (the dead giveaway that it was, as Mum feared, 'dodgy') and the steady flow of customers she seemed to know all about, even though she lived quite a few streets away from it. After the location of the dry cleaners was finally divulged, she grabbed my arm and whispered with great urgency, 'Pay cash up front, do not say hello and *do not*, under any circumstances, lose the receipt.'

'Ouch, Mum, you're hurting my arm! Why are you being so weird about this?'

'Promise me!' she begged.

'Okay, okay, I'll do all that you ask!'

So off I went armed with three of my most sparkly dresses, four black jackets with various tassels, studs and leather trimmings, and my favourite pair of black pants that sucked everything in. They were the staples of my wardrobe, as you can well imagine. I was doing a 'nucleus' clean: all the most important and utilised items put in together for a sprucing.

I now realise that was my first mistake. What was I thinking? The royal family never fly together just in case the plane goes down. The US president and vice president travel on separate planes for the same reason. You always have a spare around just in case something happens to the heir. I should have only put half of the nucleus in!

I walked in and handed over my most prized clothing possessions. The man asked for my phone number and I was then given a tiny square of pink paper and told to return the next day. I tucked the receipt away in my purse and didn't give it another thought. The next day when my youngest daughter and I fronted up to collect my clothes, I rummaged around my bag for my purse and looked for the teeny, tiny receipt.

GONE.

What? How could that be? I was so careful to put it in a safe place. Then my mother's words of warning rang in my ears: '*Do not*, under any circumstances, lose the receipt!' I had managed to do just that.

Oh well (I reassured myself) the same man is working behind the counter as yesterday, he'll remember me. It has only been twenty-four hours, after all. I approached him with my biggest, most friendly smile and said hello.

Obviously, he didn't reply. If you're keeping score I had now broken *two* of my mother's cardinal dry-cleaning rules.

The man gestured to the receipt book and requested my half of the ticket with his eyes. At this point I was forced to admit that I had, in fact, lost the piece of paper he'd given me the day before.

'I'm so sorry, I seem to have misplaced it. I thought I put it in my wallet. You remember me, right? From yesterday?'

He said, 'No receipt, no clothes.'

It was then that I noticed my clothes hanging just to the left of the counter.

I said, 'Look, they're just there, if you call the number on the receipt my phone will ring and you'll see they're mine.'

He shook his head and told me to get out.

'Can I show you some ID to prove it's me?' I pleaded.

He responded with, 'Driver's licence.'

I produced my licence, a Western Australian one as I was yet to swap back to a Victorian one.

He said, 'I do not trust this. Must be Victorian.'

I then produced:

Passport.

Medicare card.

Credit cards.

All of which bore my name and/or my resemblance.

He still refused to hand over the dresses and went on to press an alarm button that alerted the two women working out the back that trouble was brewing in the main cabin. They came rushing up to the counter demanding to know what was going on. I again tried to explain that I had lost the ticket but if *someone* would just ring the number on the receipt hanging on the dresses, my phone would ring, proving they were mine. Or perhaps they would like to peruse the fifty-five other forms of ID I had produced.

Woman number one said, 'We do not trust anything but a Victorian licence. You need to find someone with a Victorian licence to sign for you.'

What the what now? I was starting to lose my mind.

'I will not find someone with a Victorian driver's licence! I have already paid you and I have shown you more than enough forms of ID to prove who I am. I am taking my clothes and leaving!'

I picked up Odette and leant across the counter to take my clothes.

Cue the shit hitting the fan, hard.

The man behind the counter lurched at me quick as you like and had me in a headlock before I could get out the door. I still had my kid firmly on my hip but I was doubled over, trapped under the armpit of a tiny, angry man.

As this was happening woman number one jumped across the counter and LOCKED THE FUCKING DOOR!

Woman number two, with the skills of a jewel-thief-panther-ninja, managed to wrench the clothes from my hands. She screamed, 'Call the police!' to the man behind the counter.

I could *not* believe how quickly the situation had escalated. I actually looked around to see if there were hidden cameras, as surely this was an elaborate practical joke. Nope, no cameras, just three complete lunatics convinced I was trying to steal my own clothes.

So, the police were on their way and I had heard the man tell them I was 'violent' and 'angry'. Oh really? Only one person had been placed in a headlock and it wasn't any of the three small shouty people calling me a thief.

Once the door was locked and the police alerted I was finally released from the headlock and told to stand in the corner. I made a dash for the front door again, but it was locked up good and tight. I grabbed Odette, headed for the corner and called my Scotty.

Scotty: 'Hello?'

Me: '[Hiccup, sob] I'm being held captive at Mum's dry cleaners, they've called the police. They say I am trying to steal my own clothes. Can you please come, and please bring your Victorian driver's licence?'

Scotty: 'Right. [Deep sigh] I'll be there soon.'

The fact that Scotty didn't even question it or sound remotely surprised probably looks pretty bad but I can honestly say this had never happened before. Okay, so once I took on a woman who punched a bank teller in front of me but other than that my record is clean!

The police were taking their sweet time. I guess I wasn't considered that dangerous a criminal in my leopard print maxidress with my bewildered three-year-old child sitting on my hip.

Scotty arrived to find me crumpled in the corner with Odette stroking my hair. Bless her, she knew the drill. He knocked on the door and surprisingly they let him in. He produced the much sought after Victorian driver's licence and my clothes were handed over to him – JUST LIKE THAT. Once I saw that my clothes were safe and sound I unleashed a Liam Neeson–style tirade on all three of them.

'How very *dare* you, I will have you all up for assault and kidnapping. I had enough ID for goodness' sake. I will throw a brick through your window, I will make you wish you had never been born! My child will probably be scarred for life, I hope you go out of business you, fucking psychopaths!'

Of course I never followed up on any of those threats but, shit, if felt great to scream them.

Scotty bundled us out of there before the police arrived. I was shaken for some time.

When we got back to Mum and Dad's I inspected my clothes and I must say their workmanship was excellent. My vintage Chanel jacket had never looked so radiant, damn their brilliant cleaning skills!

Obviously I have never been back, but I *have* considered sending my sister in for me as no other dry cleaner has ever achieved such wonderful standards, however I dare not risk them recognising my sequinned goods.

For now I wait, brick in hand . . .

Kidding!

When I returned home after my ordeal my mother sat listening to all that had conspired with a look of horror on her face, which I naively assumed was out of concern for her grandchild and her daughter.

'What name did you give them?'

'What? Oh . . . My first name.'

'And they saw Scott's ID right? With his last name and not ours?'

'Yes . . . I guess so.'

'Right, good then.'

Mum was just grateful I hadn't given them my last name, she didn't want to be linked to me in any way for fear of them refusing to clean her wares!

After three weeks of living on top of each other things were getting desperate. We just couldn't stay at my parents' place a moment longer, so my mother sprang to action as she so often does. She found us a house, paid our bond and guaranteed the rent (bless that woman) and we were able to move into our own place almost a month after first arriving home. It had two bedrooms and was tiny but it was ours. After we got all our stuff in and the girls had settled into their new school, Scotty and I realised that we needed to think about getting jobs. While he was looking for something suitable, my glorious husband took a job at a mate's factory and rode two hours every day to get there so that I could have our only car to ferry the girls around. Scott needed to build his football contacts back up again as he had been away for so long. He has a very specific skill set and jobs at AFL football clubs – strength and conditioning ones – weren't exactly falling at his feet.

How were my job prospects looking?

In a word: FUCKED.

I was at career *ground zero*.

I was a reality-TV reject who had just walked out on a major radio station and, to put it bluntly, no bastard wanted to touch me. I was considered damaged goods, a diva, too hard and not worth the effort. My complete mental breakdown and subsequent bad behaviour in Perth had been made public knowledge by former co-hosts and other people I had worked with. I didn't know what the hell I was going to do. I had only done half a degree in interior design, had some retail experience and was a former child athlete. All I knew was singing and radio now.

I can't begin to tell you how humbling having to front up to Centrelink was when I realised we were going to need financial assistance. Just months earlier I had been on bill-boards and the backs of buses in Perth and now I required government assistance to support my family. My reality check came in swift and hard. Still, I take comfort in the fact that at no point did I think to myself, *I shouldn't have quit radio*. When a bill came in that I couldn't pay and if my mind wandered for even a second to *I used to have this money*, it would quickly correct itself and remember how bad I felt doing that job. How no amount of money was worth the constant tiredness and mental anguish I was trying to live through. The day I quit my job I wrote myself a letter, I stuck it up on the wall of wherever my stuff was and read it every day.

Take a look on the next page.

Yes, I realise there are spelling mistakes, when I write things with my hand there will ALWAYS be a spelling mistake or twenty but honestly, it lifts me up every time I read it. It reminds me that I am capable of being brave and making tough decisions that work out in the end.

Speaking of writing, it was around this time that I started up my blog (just like every girl and her dog). I had always enjoyed writing, however having a touch of the dyslexia, I found it embarrassing to share my misspelled, backwards words with anyone. But I put that fear aside and wrote every day: I wrote down my experiences, stories, hopes and dreams.

The thing is, the blog wasn't making me any sweet, sweet cash. We were barely surviving on Scott's factory

Dear Em,

Today you may be questioning your decision to quit your high paying job and return home to a lot of uncertainty.

YOU MADE THE RIGHT CHOICE!

You are now sitting at your desk after having recorded a shit/lazy/souless script for Centro Galleria.

You were abused for not delivering the correct amount of credits

You are contributing to the continual numbing and dumbing of society.

Rember how you feel now — HAPPY, RELIEVED and free.

Chin up tiger!

Em

money and I was completely at a loss as to what my next move should be.

Then Mia Freedman became aware of my blog as it was doing quite well and asked me if I would like to start contributing to her hugely successful website, Mamamia. WHAT? The girl who misspelled Australia back in Grade 2 (go back and read the intro if you skipped it) being asked to write for a website that many people actually read? Goodness me!

Would you like to read the very first thing I ever wrote for Mamamia? Of course you would! It was extremely hard hitting and cutting edge, as you can well imagine.

PLUS-SIZED MODELS ARE MAKING US FAT

(Clickbait was alive and well then – my article actually said the complete opposite!)

So here it is, ladies and gentlemen.

The reason why so many of us struggle with our weight.

The reason behind the obesity epidemic facing Western society.

Are you ready for this jelly?

The blame can be squarely laid upon the fleshy shoulders of PLUS-SIZED MODELS (can we also have a collective WTF about the fact that anyone over a size 8 is called 'plus' in the fashion world?).

Italian researchers Dr Luca Savorelli and Dr David Dragone from the University of Bologna have concluded that putting larger women on the catwalk (i.e. bigger than a size 8) sends a message to the obese people of the world that it's okay to be fat.

'To promote chubby fashion models when obesity is one of the major problems of industrialised countries seems to be a paradox . . . Given that in the US and in Europe people are on average overweight, we conclude that these policies, even when they are welfare improving, may foster the obesity epidemic.'

Of course! I bet, this very minute, thousands of over-weight people are stalking the catwalks of the world. If just ONE model dare hit the runway weighing in at more than fifty kilos they'll all rejoice. I can see them now, pumping their chubby fists in the air, screaming, 'SEE! She's a model, she's not thin, therefore I don't have to be either!'

The good 'doctors' had more truth bombs to share at the Royal Economic Society's annual conference in London this week. 'If being overweight is the average condition and the ideal body weight is thin, increasing the ideal body weight may increase welfare by reducing social pressure.'

Just so we're all clear, the 'doctors' feel we should keep our models nice and skinny so we all still aspire to be like them, thus ensuring we feel insecure about our imperfect bodies. Who needs the boring excuse of 'a better quality of life' to lose weight? We need to feel BAD about ourselves to get on the path to a healthier life.

Shame = killer abs.

For the love of all that is good and right in the world! Seriously! These men were given actual money to come up with this crap? Was this 'state sponsored' research? Silvio Berlusconi protecting his orgiastic aspirations? We CANNOT have overweight ~~hookers~~ women turning up to sex parties can we, Silvio? Even a mask won't cover that! Obviously, putting more realistic women on the catwalk WILL NOT make overweight people feel good about being overweight. What a breathtakingly ridiculous statement. Putting 'larger' models on the catwalk would be a HUGE step in the right direction. I could bleat on about 'realistic role models' and 'positive body image' but anyone with half a brain knows why 'real women' on a runway would be a better situation for everyone.

Back to our friends from Italy. I am confused as to why they were concerned about this issue to begin with. Has there been a dramatic increase in overweight models that I am unaware of and did this increase coincide with a spike in the world's obesity rates? No, no, there hasn't been. In fact, models are thinner than ever and obesity rates are the highest they've ever been. I didn't need a degree from the University of Bologna to figure out that either.

Back to the drawing board, dottores.

Oh *boom*! So sassy! Thanks, Em!

So now I was a proper writer! Well, sort of. I was still chronically unemployed and seriously lacking in any direction. One night after dinner, Scotty and I were in the kitchen cleaning up and I was complaining about being bored and feeling useless when he said to me, 'Well, what is your dream job? What would you be doing if you could just click your fingers and make it happen?'

I thought about it and replied, 'I'd tell stories, sing and write.'

'So why don't you do that?'

'Do what?'

'Tell stories, sing and write . . . Write your own show. If you build it they will come.'

'Did you just quote *Field of Dreams*?'

'Yes, but you're missing the point. You need to go out and find your people.'

Bloody hell, he was right. The very next day I sat down and started writing my first ever stand-up/cabaret/ confessional therapy stage show. Did I have any idea how to do that? Of course not! That didn't stop me from having a crack at singing, radio, writing and TV.

Let's find out how Blog Em was feeling about putting on her first ever show! (Hint: I think the title is more than self-explanatory.)

DEAR GOD WHAT HAVE I DONE?

Who the hell do I think I am? I mean really. It all seemed like such a good idea at the time, something I could totally pull off. Now, I'm having anxiety and regret of such epic proportions I'm finding it hard to breathe/sleep/function.

What have I done? Oh I'll tell you what I've done . . . No, I don't think I can bring myself to type the words for fear of asphyxiating on the fumes of impending failure. (Dramatic enough for you?)

Oh all right.

You'll need to read this next paragraph in a fast, high-pitched, slightly manic voice and try not to breathe. (This is how it loops in my head.)

I've booked in a venue for my one-woman show and now I have to sell tickets and I'm afraid no one will turn up except Mum and Dad, who will be there out of obligation. I'm also concerned that I will sell tickets therefore people will be expecting to be entertained only what if I can't be entertaining? What if my voice can't hack the gruelling eight pop songs a night? What if people find my stories self-indulgent and boring? Oh God, what have I done?

Yes, I'm aware this entire line of thought is self-indulgent. Yes, I'm aware doing a one-woman show telling stories about my life is pretty self-indulgent also but bear with me, folks, I'm a woman ON THE EDGE.

I've ceased 'the sleeping' all together. Anxiety pretty much consumes me and I am convinced I have taken on far too much. So, all is pretty normal!

That being said, I am really looking forward to performing. The experience of doing something that scares the shit out of me and also allowing me to combine my love of telling stories and music has been a fantastic one.

Here is the show poster:

If you think you can spare the time to come to one of the shows I'd really love to see you there. All my friends and family are coming (out of obligation), however it would be great to see some new faces as well.

A lot of you would only have ever seen me in thirty second bursts on The 7PM Project *or perhaps remember me from* Idol *when, well, I wasn't really sure what the hell I was doing. (I am marginally better now!)*

If you're curious please come along.

OH BOY. She was pretty anxious, wasn't she? You can actually smell the desperation in her words. I wish I could go back and tell Blog Em that it all works out for the absolute best and that now we are writing a proper book with a fancy publisher and putting on shows in largish theatres. *The Saintly Bitch Sings* went for four nights, I played it to twenty-five people each night and I am happy to report for the first time ever in my life, I was proud of myself. Charlie Pickering (clever comedian and TV host) had also been encouraging me in the background. At the time I was doing the 'Metro Whip Around' for *The 7PM Project* on Channel 10. He was the host and I had confessed to him that I was going to try doing musical comedy and he was so bloody supportive. Truly marvelous. I am sure he wouldn't remember this, but his pep talks and weekly inquiries as to how the show was progressing really helped me at the time. Then he actually showed up on opening night in the tiny room that I was performing in and laughed the loudest – CAN YOU EVEN? What a guy, eh? The show went so well that I decided to write another one and enter it into the Melbourne International Comedy Festival, because that is the kind of ridiculous shit I like to do.

Things were really starting to look up for me career wise so of course it was at about this time that the wheels well and truly fell off my marriage.

13

Separation

If I was to be completely honest, Scotty and I probably shouldn't have made it past the first month of our relationship; we started arguing very early on and continued to do it with vigour for the next twelve years. It's just that we were crazy about one another and that always seemed to win out over the fighting. Oh, and the sex was spectacular, thanks for not asking.

Our relationship had been tested on many, many occasions. Things had never been easy for us. We'd not known each other long before I fell pregnant, so we didn't get to properly 'date' one another. Instead of boozy trips to Bali we were choosing jogging prams, Baby Björns and genuinely having the cloth vs disposable nappy debate.

HAWT.

We had moved interstate three times, had two kids, survived my depression, his unemployment, *my* unemployment and numerous extended family dramas. We were a team. A somewhat dysfunctional one, but a team nonetheless.

He was my family.

He got me.

He accepted me after he got me.

He was kind when I was fragile.

He advised me.

He stood up for me.

He loved me. Which I accept probably wasn't and still isn't always easy.

I thought we'd be together forever.

It all fell apart in November 2012. We were well and truly broken and completely out of bandaids. We were getting to the stage where each time I walked in the door I had to try to remember if we were on speaking terms or not.

We usually weren't.

Separating was a horrible, slow and painful process. It took Scotty until February 2013 to move out. We were both terrified to let go but at the same time desperately wanted to. Christmas was a horrifying ordeal, and then we inexplicably decided to go on one last family holiday together. Yes, how Gwenyth Paltrow/Chris Martin of us. On a side note, am I the only one who hopes that after they 'consciously uncoupled' Chris went and secretly snuck gluten into all the food in her fridge and then went out and ate a rare steak off the crotch of an exotic dancer?

Needless to say, the end of my marriage hit me hard. We had decided on the course of action together, yes, we really had. Even so, deep down, I didn't think it would actually happen. I confess to feeling like I'd failed as a woman, because I couldn't keep my man. It's always the lady who has to 'keep' the man, isn't it? Like we've managed to trap a rare exotic bird and if we don't do the exact right thing, it will die.

Like my marriage did.

My marriage was a dead rare exotic bird.

Seriously though, if I may put my Sasha Fierce hat on for a moment (that is a Beyoncé reference and if you don't get it, what are you even doing here?), society teaches girls that the real measure for success is marriage. If you can find a man to want you enough to make it legal, then you've done all right. I am trying very hard to teach my girls that marriage is an option and not the end game. Similar to the way a lot of men approach the female orgasm. AMIRITE, ladies? YEAH, UP TOP!

Telling the girls their dad and I were separating was a special kind of pain to experience. I didn't really know how to do it – I'd only ever seen it done on the TV. I knew we were supposed to say things like 'It's not your fault' and 'Dad and I love you both very much' and 'Who do you love most?'. Yet here is how the scene played out.

SCOTT AND EM'S SEPARATION SCENE

Scott and Em sit opposite each other on a pair of extremely tasteful, vintage lounge-room chairs that Em had obviously picked for the house with love and care.

Em

Girls, can you come into the lounge room please, your dad and I need to talk to you.

Marchella

Coming!

Odette

Coming!

Fifteen minutes pass. It is clear the girls are not coming as they said they were. Scott begins pacing the lounge room, Em arranges the extremely tasteful cushions that adorn the magnificent couches. They are uncomfortable around each other, there is no eye contact.

Scott

GIRLS! NOW!

Marchella

Okay, we're coming, keep your jocks on, mate.

Odette

What's wrong? Did the dog poo on the rug again? I am not picking that up. It's Chella's turn.

Separation

Marchella

It is not! Is Dad gay? Is that what you're telling us? Congratulations, I'm glad you can finally be you.

Note to reader, there is a running joke within my family stemming from an episode of The Simpsons *where Homer suggests Lisa signs a card that reads: P.S I am gay. Scott and I write that on all the notes and cards we give to the girls. In any other circumstances, this would have been an excellent call-back joke by Marchella.*

Note re note: NOT that we think it's a joke to be homosexual. As you've already discovered, I am a fierce champion and friend of the LGBTQI community.

Em

No, Chella. Dad and I have decided to take a break for a little while. I'm staying here with you guys and Dad will go and live at Nana's house. I'm very sorry. We're both very sorry.

End scene. . .

They both looked at me and I think they could sense the immense pain I was in. They didn't react as I'd expected them to. Odette, who was seven at the time, said, 'That's okay, Mummy, we will still see you both. We love you. Will you teach Dad to do my hair? He can't do my hair. I'm hungry. What's for dinner?'

That's my Odie – fashion and food before a fall.

My eldest didn't say much at all, she just sat there fighting back tears. I tried to give her a hug but she shrugged it off and briskly went to her room. Her silence terrified me. Marchella has never not had anything to say. I was prepared for anger and tears, not stoic silence. She was struggling.

The day Scotty moved out I remember being consumed by worry.

I worried that I would be alone for the rest of my life.

I worried that I was scarring my children irrevocably.

I worried that he would start seeing someone straight-away who was pretty and smart and had perky tits and a flat stomach.

I worried about someone else seeing me naked.

I worried that my heart would feel torn apart until the end of time.

Most of all I worried about him.

The nights were the worst. During the day I was brave and made plans. In the evenings it would all dissolve and I would find myself in bed at 2am, hatching ways to win him back.

I tried to stay in our house but I kept running into memories. Wedding photos, anniversary cards, our children. It was like a really tragic episode of *Hoarders*. (So every episode of *Hoarders* really.) On a side note, if you ever feel like the housework has gotten away from you, washing piling up, etc, just watch an episode of that show and you will feel like fucking Mary Poppins. Those people find dead cats under their shit, not just odd socks, DEAD FUCKING CATS. I spent a lot of my time smelling Scotty's pillow, refusing to wash his dirty undies and at one low point considered collecting his pubes to crochet a comforting rug with. I was in what I now refer to as the DEFCON-one-Adele phase of the break-up.

Oh, Adele. Where would the modern woman be without Adele's music to cry and masturbate to? Except *Skyfall*, M died in that and there is nothing sexy about Dame Judi Dench getting a bullet through her heart. Separated from Scotty, I went into a death roll with Adele's album *21*. I felt like every single song had been written directly for me and my pain. I had it on high rotation. You know when you convince yourself that you are in the worst pain of anyone ever, no-one has ever been this heartbroken and survived? The trouble is now I can't hear an Adele song without thinking of that time. Marchella had a piano recital shortly after her father moved out and as a surprise she learned a few Adele songs to play for me. She told the audience the songs were 'special to Mum, they are the ones she likes to listen to alone in her room every night'. I was about five glasses of red in and half a hipflask down and had to smile as I fought the urge to slide off my seat.

I tried to do some things to make the space my own. I even purchased a brand-new bed for all the sex I would be having with all the new guys I was defiantly going to be meeting to have sex with in my new bed. The trouble was I only slept on my side – his side was always made and on the bedside table there was still the plate he'd had his toast on the morning he'd moved out.

I soldiered on. Thankfully I had full-time work to keep me going. Dave Cameron (you may know him as Hamish and Andy's boss 'Grumpy Dave') approached me and said that he enjoyed my columns on Mamamia and thought perhaps they would extend to a great radio show. I was hesitant to go anywhere near radio again – I got a stress rash when the idea was first suggested – however I was told I could pick my co-host and could start work at noon each day and be out in time to get the girls from school. SOLD! Comedian Dave Thornton was my first pick and the Mamamia Today radio show was born. It aired nationally from 3 to 4pm and I really enjoyed doing it. I adored Dave Thornton, we were pretty much left to our own devices, and it completely restored my faith in radio.

So, as long as I had my girls, my sense of humour and my high-paying enjoyable job in radio I would possibly be okay! Then one Friday afternoon, after we'd finished a show, I saw Dave Cameron coming towards the studio. That was never a good sign. As I saw him striding down the hallway, I did a quick audit of the show just gone to check I hadn't said anything untoward. You see, there had been an incident the week before where at the start of the show I had said, 'Take a knee, Australia, get around us, it's going to be a rad show.' Unfortunately that was not what my boss had heard and I found myself being asked why I had told Australia to 'take an E'. As in an ecstasy tablet. Baby Jesus wept in heaven – what a day that was. It appears my boss has never watched a sporting movie in his life, or heard any type of inspirational speech. Radio, huh? Whacky times. My left eye is twitching for some reason . . .

So as my boss walked into the studio followed by his second-in-command, I wondered what was going on. One look at both their faces and I instantly knew.

No more radio show.

Usually in these situations I get rather emotional. Dave Thornton and I had put in a lot of hard work and we were very proud of the show. I loved doing the show, I loved the people I worked with and, let's face it, the income was useful as well. As our boss explained the reasons we were no longer going to air (which appeared to be purely financial and not a reflection of the quality of the product), instead of wanting to lash out and fight, I accepted it. Trust me, no-one was as surprised at this turn of events than me. Imagine if instead of throwing the phone at the police officer's head, Naomi Campbell had offered to use the phone to ring his mother and tell her what a good job she had done with raising him – such was the level of shift in my behaviour.

So the show wrapped up shortly after and then they rehired Dave, gave him a national weekend breakfast show, and replaced me with Sophie Monk.

Yep.

Feel the fucking burn.

The bad thing about that besides the fact I was no longer employed is that Sophie was exactly who I imagined my husband would be replacing me with: blonde, hot, great rack.

So I started irrationally hating Sophie Monk. She had been on a reality singing show too, so my husband obviously had a type!

I know Sophie a bit now and I think she is a pretty solid bird. She doesn't take herself too seriously, is a bit of a dag and hilariously funny, but at the time I HATED HER. It was the kind of irrational hatred that, if I was carrying the washing and I heard her voice on the radio, I would have to put the washing down so that I could hate her with my whole body. I managed to convince myself that Sophie Monk was the reason my life was going down the toilet. I had also convinced myself that Scott was probably at that very moment fucking her in a hotel and they were laughing at me and calling me fat. Of course that was just my fevered imagination, but that didn't stop me from leaving 'constructive criticism' on Fox FM's Facebook page. It didn't take long for 'Donna from Frankston' to get banned from commenting.

Being unemployed and heartbroken was not a great mix.

I actually googled 'how to deal with heartbreak', I was so desperate. Experts recommend that you avoid alcohol, pills and drugs during this time. That you should exercise and look after you. Experts are stupid jerks. Oh GOD I've just found our wedding album – I know what will make me feel better! A brisk jog. FUCK THAT. Pour me all the wine and pass me my shot gun, I'm going to sit on the front veranda and point it at anyone who smiles.

I was feeling so bad I took myself off to my doctor, hoping there was a 'freshly separated' pill.

Dr G took one look at me and said, 'Has he gone?'

I managed a nod. He then proceeded to write me two prescriptions: one for the Pill and one for Valium, so I was covered if I wanted to get fucked or be fucked. He is a good man.

I lasted about four months in the house after Scott moved out before I realised I couldn't do it anymore. I called my dad and whimpered, 'I think it might be time for me to move out.'

Dad sprang into action, organising a moving truck, AKA his mate Boz (called that because he is Bosnian – thank God he wasn't Nigerian). I had three weeks exactly to pack up. The thing is, I just couldn't bring myself to pack up the home. To a stranger it still looked like a happy family of four lived there; putting it all in boxes felt like the final death.

The day before the truck was due to arrive, Dad called me to check we were on track.

'I'm having a little trouble packing,' I confessed between sobs.

Dad drove over to find me, sobbing, surrounded by boxes, wearing my – can you guess? Yes, I was the perfectly scorned woman cliché resplendent in my wedding dress! On a shallow side note though, the wedding dress was *swimming* on me. I was miserable but I was thin due to anxiety, so every cloud and all that.

Dad just started shoving things in boxes. 'If I can pack up sixty years of your grandfather,' he said to me, 'you can do this. Just look at it as a job.'

Oh! Low emotional blow, Vincie! Way to bring our beloved dead father/grandfather into the equation to make me realise how pathetic I was being. You see, my Grandpa Luigi came here in 1953 with his three brothers, Guissepe, Giovanni and Antonio. Their sister Maria stayed in Italy. My Dad and Nona came across to join him in 1954. They lived on Lygon Street (of course they did) until 1956 and bought their house in Coburg in 1958. After just two years in the country! Needless to say they paid cash for it. It was decorated in fifties Euro chic and wasn't touched for 60 years. When we packed up his place in Coburg after he passed away we found jars of seeds he smuggled here from Italy because he didn't trust Australian seeds. So Dad packed and I lit small grass fires and tore strips off my wedding dress to fuel them. Dad got sick of my hiccupping so he sent me out for a walk. I WAS STILL WEARING THE WEDDING DRESS.

The next time I was at the house it was completely empty. Nothing. A once busy, happy house now empty. I went and purchased an industrial-sized bottle of hospital-grade Domestos and I bleached the pain away. The house represented me and it's possible the bleach represented the amount of alcohol I had begun consuming to erase all traces of Scott from my brain.

So we moved in with my mum and dad. I was not in a great way mentally and probably should not have been making major life decisions like, say, which school my youngest daughter should be attending after we moved suburbs. I just picked the one closest to us, without doing my homework. Odie *loved* her old school. She was king of the kids, and everyone in the school knew her and loved her. Why wouldn't they? She is a rad kid, ask anyone. It was a lovely school, they would paint pictures of their feelings, grow vegies and knot tampons for needy children.

Quite seriously, my youngest has a special magic that lives inside of her. She's sensitive, creative and wired slightly differently to most. But two weeks into her attending her new school, I was convinced I had destroyed her magic. You see, my lovely little girl was having trouble making friends, and by that I mean no bastard would play with her. Every night she would look at me with her big blue eyes and tearfully ask if she had to go school the next day. Oh God, *the pain*. Not to be too dramatic about it but it felt like someone had broken my heart into a bazillion pieces, set it on fire, put it out with acid, ate it, shat it out and then put it through a wood chipper. Part of me wanted to respond with 'Of course not, honey! We can go to the park, eat tiny delicate sandwiches and frolic with nature.' Instead I responded with variations of 'Yes, babes, it'll be better tomorrow.'

We tried different things. On her first day she marched up to a few kids and asked if she could play with them. That's Odie, brave and open. She was shut down each time with one girl telling her, 'We don't have room for anyone else.' What the what now?

I know these little kids are only seven, I get that they didn't yet completely comprehend the full awesomeness of my kid but still, bloody hell! That shit be brutal! Odie would come home devastated. I wanted to go and find those kids and speak very firmly to them in a non-intimidating but slightly scary manner. I felt helpless, guilty and sad. I didn't want this to change her, I didn't want it to alter the way she saw the world. She was still full of wonder and love but her spirit was slowly being crushed by the oppressors in the playground. I knew things were bad because she had stopped singing, and my kid sings more than she talks. All day, every day, she trills. She is very good; not only is it pleasant, it is a helpful way to keep track of her.

Odie thought that maybe if she got her hair cut and some groovy purple streaks put in this would gain her some mates. So we did it. I would pretty much have bought her a solid gold unicorn and led her around the playground on it if that would've helped in any way.

I also found out she had been buying some kids lollies at the canteen with her pocket money in an attempt to win them over. I may not have even cared if that had worked! But no dice.

HEARTBREAKING.

I desperately tried to keep my shit together, and tried to not be a psychotic, hovering helicopter mum, but you don't know! You didn't see the big teary blue eyes at night, you didn't see the slow walk to school with the head down or my baby wandering alone at lunch time. We stuck it out for as long as possible, I even volunteered to do the class reading. That didn't last too long – I once dared to take the children out into the sunshine to read because the class-room smelled of sweaty tweens, a heady combination of warm yeast and cheese. Someone saw me outside with the kids and dobbed me in to the principal. Apparently you're not allowed to take children away from their classroom, even if it's just two metres, as the teacher can't supervise you. I was called into the principal's office and my working with children check demanded. It was all very upsetting. I was just trying to make things a little better for Odie and her classmates. Eventually we moved schools again, and things are much better now. She is at a place that truly appreciates her unique nature and hair colours. Plus it's the same school her older sister goes to, and no one messes with Marchella. Not even her father and I!

After the school reading incident I set about making my personal life infinitely worse by attempting to win my husband back. It started innocently enough. My parents were away and I knew he was coming to pick the girls up, so I arranged for the children to be out of the house when he arrived. Obviously I opened the door in a nurse's uniform. You know, the usual custody access visit.

I seduced him.

He never stood a chance.

We started hanging out, going on dates. We were both living with our parents so it was like being teenagers again.

We even went jogging together around the Tan. Yes, we were those people, shut up, don't judge. He started coming to the girls' athletics and gymnastics with me. We were a semi-family once more.

One day after a couples jog, I said to him, 'So when do you think you and I can start looking for a house to live in?'

He looked at me with a mixture of panic and pity and said, 'What do you mean? We're not getting back together. Nothing has changed. *Nothing has changed.*'

That's when I finally realised, we were really finished. Obviously, for me, the first break up didn't really happen. You know when you end it with someone and the only thing truly keeping you going is the smug knowledge that they will eventually see the error of their ways and come crawling back to you? As Scott got in his car, I stood there in shock and, in a daze, watched the other sickeningly happy couples jog around me. I couldn't believe it, he was walking away, and not once looking back. It was at that point that it finally hit me that we were never getting back together . . . Well, not for another year at least!

So I decided it would be a good idea to throw myself into dating. Christ, dating as a single mother in your thirties is comparable to what I imagine competing in the Hunger Games to be: you'll find yourself wanting to cut a bitch should she get between you and a good dude! I did manage to find one I quite liked, though. We'd met at a food and wine festival and he seemed like a goer. I liked him enough to allow things to progress to an at-home DVD date. To get my body match-fit I needed an entire day's preparation. This was next level stuff, y'all. I even went to the trouble of shaving down like a greyhound preparing for her next race. (Wait, do greyhounds shave down? I've never seen a bald greyhound. You get the drift though.) I did the matching underwear thing and sprayed perfume on my hard-to-reach areas, I even checked my nipples for the presence of bubes.

I had generously allowed him to pick the movie and vowed to myself that I wouldn't judge him on his choice. This excluded snuff movies, hardcore porn or anything starring Rob Schneider – I simply could not transcend negative evaluation should any of the above occur.

Turns out the DVD he presented me with was much, much worse.

As I'd not seen this particular film and only had the title to go by, I thought it sounded fun. I imagined a fantasy movie. I pictured a heroine with billowing golden hair and a most excellent velvet frock. I felt a white horse with equally luscious follicles would be involved, possibly a handsome man and definitely a few sassy woodland creatures.

I deduced all of this from the title of the DVD: *Requiem for a Dream.*

What? It had the word 'dream' in it!

For those of you who *have* seen it, I imagine you've had some sort of violent physical reaction to me revealing the title of the movie he chose for our date. For those of you who haven't seen it, let me give you a brief synopsis.

Starring Jared Leto and Jennifer Connolly, *Requiem for a Dream* is the delightful (read: catastrophically horrific) story of four addicts. Their problems range from hard drugs to self-help shows. Over the course of the film the characters' lives slowly descended to shit. I mean it, there's no happy ending; this film starts bad and ends even worse. The final ten minutes is *the most traumatic* passage of film in the history of the world ever.

SPOILER ALERT.

Jared Leto's character is having his needle track-ridden arm sawn off while Jennifer Connolly's character is forced to have anal sex with a very frightening lady and her giant double-ended dildo. This is phased in and out with the other main character stuck in prison inexplicably mixing mashed potatoes in a giant pot. Then we cross to Jared's character's elderly mother (the game-show addict) getting electric shock therapy. Back to Jared, who is completely sans arm then flash to mash potato guy spewing into the pot and then EVERYONE IS DEAD.

After it finished we sat there in a strange silence. I felt shell-shocked. There is no other way to put it: I felt raw, frightened and damaged. This is not one of those movies you can move on from once the credits roll. It actually messes with your DNA.

I didn't know what to say as the situation was approaching a level of weirdness even I had never encountered, and as I looked over at my date, the evening managed to completely insert itself into wrongtown.com.

How do I put this delicately? He was at attention. Wooded. Aroused. Oh God, there was a party in his pants all up in his junk, and I was the guest of honour.

What the actual what? I mean the cinematography was beautiful but bloody hell, really? *That* is what got him going? Guys, I realise I haven't dated since the late nineties but that's not cool – right? Why did this bloke feel that was the kind of movie we should be watching together? I mean, I wasn't expecting *The Notebook* but surely something like *Empire Records* or, I don't know, *any other movie* that didn't involve the forceful removal of limbs, rape or spewing into mashed root vegies.

Am I looking too deeply into this? Was he just trying to widen my cinematic experiences or was he a potential serial killer who had a woven coat made from strands of my hair hidden away?

I made a graceful exit . . . 'Something something . . . I think I may need deep psychological therapy after this . . . something . . . I'll call you.'

Anyway, funny-slash-disturbing stuff, hey?

I stopped dating after that and stated hanging out with my parents on Saturday nights. Things were pretty grim. One night I caught a glimpse of myself reflected on the TV screen sitting between them on the couch during a break in the *West Wing* marathon we were having and knew something needed to change. So I stated writing a show called *Divorce, the Musical!*. I figured there were other women out there going through something similar to me and why shouldn't we be able to laugh at our misery and sing songs to accompany it. The problem was, my guitarist Ryan was preparing to move away to Canada to be with the love of his life. I know: selfish. So I had a show but no guitarist.

One night after cooking me dinner, Dad gently suggested that he would be happy to play guitar for me if I'd like. I wouldn't have to pay him, just make sure he had a light beer before each gig. Dad knew I needed to get out of the house and back working again.

So I did. We did. That moment was my dad saying to me not only that he would work for free but that I could do life again. Because of Vincie, I survived one of the most emotionally challenging times of my life, and let's be honest – there have been a few! He single handedly moved me out of my house, took me into his and then gave me my career back.

Around the time Dad agreed to step in and play guitar for me, a friend stepped in and gave me some serious, life-changing help. Without his assistance I wouldn't have been able to turn things around. This particular pal is someone you may know, he is a fellow *Australian Idol* alumnus. Although, when we first met, I wanted nothing to do with him as he was very busy being the country's most eligible bachelor AKA sleaze bag, and at the same time was courting Paris Hilton.

Yes.

Rob 'Millsy' Mills.

For those of you not sure who he is: Rob was on the first season of *Idol*, he was a shell-necklace wearing, blond tip–sporting pants man. When we arrived for the second season of *Australian Idol* the stories about Millsy were legendary among the crew, to them he was a horny demigod.

I'm not going to steal his thunder though (my lawyer just breathed a huge sigh of relief), no doubt he'll have a book out one of these days – let's face it, they're giving those things out like Oprah on a sugar high hosting her Christmas special. *YOU* GET A BOOK DEAL! AND *YOU* GET A BOOK DEAL! AND *YOU* GET A BOOK DEAL! BOOOOOOOOOOOOOOOK DEEEEEEEAL!

Rob stalked me on social media for a few years, telling me that we absolutely needed to be friends, that I had him all wrong, that we made sense together! I relented in the end and he became my rock. He is in the select group of people I would call if I had accidentally killed someone and needed help. And his big act of love came two years into our friendship in 2013.

I was visiting Rob in Elwood, where he was staying with his friend Trish while he was in Melbourne perform-ing in *Wicked*. The girls were with Scott for the weekend so I was blowing in the wind; I didn't have much work on so without them I had very little purpose. To put things into context, Marchella had just started at her new high school, and while she had received a scholarship, I still had to come up with half the tuition. My car repayments were behind, my phone had been barred and I had three credit cards maxed out trying to keep up. I was living with Mum and Dad but didn't want to ask them for financial help as they were doing enough. I felt completely out of control and helpless, and as I was walking towards Rob's house, my dad called to say that a childhood friend's mother had died. I hadn't seen her in many years, however this woman had been like a mother to me when I was growing up, and I spent a lot of time at her house – most weekends, in fact. The thought of her suddenly not being in the world, leaving her loving, tight-knit family, who I knew would be completely devastated at her passing, took my breath away.

I was already fragile before the phone call, lonely and missing the girls. Finding out that this woman had passed away broke what little bravery I had left and I sat on the footpath in front of Rob's house and cried. More accurately, I sobbed, until I had a projectile snot situation all up in my nose. It was the middle of the day and I was basically spread-eagled on the footpath, melting down with reckless abandon.

Rob and his girlfriend Ellen pulled up about five minutes after I'd begun the breakdown. They got out of the car and rushed over to see what had happened. They both sat and patiently listened as I admitted everything, in weird, broken, hiccupy sentences. I rambled and they made sense of how behind I was in life, in love and in my finances. That I wasn't sure what was next, that I felt I was letting my girls down, that a woman who had played a big part in raising me was now dead. It was a lot for them to take in. Robbie walked me inside and Ellen went off to find sugary treats – she had read the play well and knew we needed some time alone. Robbie made me a cup of tea, then he asked how he could best help me. I said I didn't know, that perhaps I was beyond help.

He asked me what I was most worried about, to which I replied, 'The money, I just can't keep up. I don't want Chella to have to move schools, I need my car – I just can't get any work at the moment.'

'What if I took care of the money situation?'

'No.'

'Em, I have plenty of money, what's the point if I can't help the people I love?'

'No, I can't do it. I don't like owing people anything. It would haunt me. Besides, Rob, we're talking thousands of dollars.'

'How much exactly?'

'That's the terrifying thing – I have no idea. I'm too scared to find out.'

'Well . . . Let's check together.'

So we sat at his laptop and went through my finances one bill at a time. I was $16 000 in debt. I nearly passed out.

'We're just going to pay them all, you can pay me back whenever you can. I don't care how long it takes. You're worth it, and things are going to turn around for you. You are too talented for it not to. This is an investment in you.'

I started crying all over again. Sometimes all it takes is just one other person to look you in the eye and say that they believe in you to spark the return of a tiny bit of self-belief. So he paid off Marchella's school fees, my overdue car instalments, my phone bill, my tax bill and all my credit cards in one sitting. My gratitude was overwhelming. I felt instantly lighter.

The guilt hit me hard a few minutes after, of course, however for a few glorious seconds I was swimming again instead of drowning and desperately trying to hang on.

I have now paid him back every cent. It took me two and a half years but I did it. He never once held it over my head or demanded the money back when I would go months without paying him. He believed in me at a time I desperately needed it and it paid off. That was a huge turning point for me, so Robbie, if I haven't said it enough: I appreciate it, I love you and I thank you.

Scotty and I did eventually come back together at the beginning of 2014. We put a huge bandaid over all our issues (warning, warning, warning) and fell back into marriage again. Both of us were missing each other terribly, the girls wanted their dad home and I couldn't live with Mum and Dad a second longer. So, we agreed to go to counselling together and rented a place near the girls' school. I felt so much relief having him home, I no longer had to worry about him or the permanent damage I may or may not have been doing to our children. The counselling helped for a little while, until we stopped going, because well . . .

My life exploded, as you're about to read.

14

Em, I've Got Something to Tell You

I'm not sure how to write this particular chapter. I know that I want the words to be the most lovely, poignant and meaningful I've ever conjured up. I want them to sit heavily on the page so that you understand how important they are to me. I'm already sobbing onto my keyboard, as I know what is to come. The events that you're going to read about took me to the very outer limits of the human experience. I was tearing along the edge of emotional oblivion like a wrung-out desperado while they were unfolding. They were also the catalyst for a great shift in me: from enormous grief I found a strength and purpose I didn't know I possessed.

These events made me brave, they enabled me to let go of all the insignificant crap I was carrying around and, afterwards, I was able to get on with the business of living. I will do my best to recount them in an honest and respectful way.

So here goes.

On Sunday 12 October 2014, I got one of those phone calls where time speeds up and stands still all at once. One of those phone calls that focuses the world around you down to a tiny pinpoint. One of those phone calls that started with 'Em, I've got some bad news.'

If you've ever received this type of phone call, and I am sure that many of you have, then you know everything that happens after that becomes a bit of a blur. Your coping mechanisms take over as you attempt to continue functioning and remembering how to breathe.

My mother's youngest sister Rachael explained to me that my Uncle Haydn, her brother, had been involved in a horrific car accident driving back from his son's, my cousin Brendan's, wedding. Through a fog I heard her explain that he'd fallen asleep at the wheel, that he was still alive but that there had been some spinal damage. His wife, my Aunty Alva, had seen the whole thing. She was driving behind him, as they'd taken separate cars the day before due to differing work schedules. Alva had looked on in horror as she saw Haydn's car veer off the road and flip over. Alva was able to flag down a passing car and call an ambulance. Uncle Haydn was airlifted to the Alfred

Hospital in Melbourne, and as most of the family were up in Albury where the wedding had been, there were only a few of us in Melbourne to meet the chopper so my mother and I went to the hospital to wait for him. My Uncle Russ (Mum's other brother) drove Alva down to Melbourne with his wife Irene. I can't even begin to fathom what Alva went through in the three excruciating hours it took her to get to her husband.

As I sat in the ICU waiting room I wondered about all the other people there and what had happened to their person. We all had the same worried expressions on our faces. The ICU waiting room seldom brings good news – it's a solemn, heavy place. Finally Uncle Russ, Aunty Irene and Aunty Alva arrived and she was able to go in and see Uncle Haydn. He was still unconscious and there really had been no developments with his condition since he'd arrived. Hours passed and I began to obsessively study the faces of the nurses going in and out of his room, looking for some clue as to what his prognosis was.

After a seemingly endless amount of time, his doctor came out and gestured for all of us to gather in a nearby conference room. I studied his face and instantly knew the news wasn't good. My mother, Uncle Russ and Aunty Irene, Aunty Alva and I sat down around a table in a sparsely decorated room. I noticed a single box of tissues sitting in the middle of the table, a presumptuous decorating choice, yet a necessary one, I was sure. The space felt heavy, and I could feel the sadness of countless families in it; this was the bad news place. Somewhere people could go to quietly lose their shit while maintaining a shred of dignity. I've never wanted to leave a room more in my life. It was suffocating. I wanted to kick down the door the instant my mother shut it behind her.

Haydn's doctor looked around the table for the leader, someone to deliver the information to, someone to ask questions of him, someone to take control of the situation of behalf of Haydn's family. I looked around the table too and saw that everyone had their heads bowed, they were all at their absolute threshold of emotion. No one wanted to ask him, because asking him set the truth into motion and deep down we all knew that truth was not going to be pleasant.

So I started asking questions. I shut down every feeling I had and I went to a place that may have seemed cold and callous at the time, but it was the only way I could get through the conversation.

'How is he?'

'He is still unconscious, we are starting to bring him around now.'

'How is his spine?'

'Not good, it has extensive damage.'

'What does that mean?'

'At this stage, it is very unlikely that Haydn will have any feeling from the neck down.'

'Ever?'

'No.'

'Is he going to live?'

'At this stage we are still assessing his injuries and will have more information as the night progresses. He requires a ventilator to breathe – we do not expect that situation to change either.'

'Ever?'

'No.'

'So you are sure about the quadriplegia?'

'Yes.'

'Does he know?'

'No.'

Those words were truly unreal. You hear about this kind of thing, see it on TV, but you never think you'll be on the end of one of those phone calls and then sitting in intensive care at 3am being told by an exhausted, impossibly young doctor that someone you love is in such a bad state.

My immediate concern was for my aunty, his wife. Up until this point she had been a tower of strength – powerfully stoic, for lack of a better term. As the news began to sink in, I watched as finally she crumbled, huge, heaving sobs wracking her body. She kept saying that Haydn wouldn't want to live, that he has always said that if this type of thing were to happen to him he wouldn't want to be trapped in his body. He was a farmer, a bus driver, a motorbike enthusiast, a fisherman, a hunter, a fireman, a footballer; he used every inch of his body every day. He'd also had a very close mate injured in a motorbike accident who had become paralysed and so he'd thought long and hard about that particular set of circumstances should it ever happen to him.

My Uncle Russ was in shock, so was his wife, and my mum sat quietly not saying a word. All the while, Alva raged, 'Why is this happening?'

I excused myself from the room and walked the empty corridors of the hospital. Counting my steps and breaths, noticing the scuffs on the linoleum, listening to the beeping of the machines, I tried to stay present so as not to be too overwhelmed with the situation. I wanted to stay calm for my Aunty Alva. I wanted to be alert and steady for when my cousins Brendan and Evan (Haydn's sons) arrived. I also wanted to be able to ask the right questions of the doctors when and if I was needed to do so again.

The next day (Monday) Haydn's boys arrived and so did the rest of my family. All of Denise and Ted Spence's five kids were in the same place at the same time, which was an extremely rare occurrence. Like any family, they had their issues, some long standing and some fresh, but one of their own was in need and so they put their feelings aside and sat in solidarity in the ICU waiting room.

As the week went on it became obvious to all that my uncle was not going to make it, and his condition was fast deteriorating, his body unable to cope with the extent of his injuries. I was finally able to talk to him on the Friday, five days after the accident. He'd been moved to palliative care at the Austin Hospital. I walked into the ward a little bit frightened, not knowing what to expect. I knew that he was completely aware of his situation, what I didn't know was what I should say to him. I decided to honour our relationship and just be honest, blunt and real as that was the way he and I had always communicated.

I pushed the blue curtain out of the way and walked into his cubicle. They had his bed raised up so he was in a seated position and he had tubes coming out of everywhere. He had pressure bandages around his limbs and his skin had a yellowish tinge to it. Then I noticed his face was bloated and I started to panic. I wasn't sure I wanted to see him now, but then he looked at me with his unbelievably blue eyes and nothing else mattered. There he was, the man who had given me my first ever beer. The man who had let me swear in front of him as a kid and who'd taught me how to shoot a gun and ride a motorbike. He stared at me and our eyes locked onto each other. I wanted to look away as it was utterly overwhelming but I didn't, I held his gaze. After a time he almost seemed to be looking through me, he looked at me in such a way that it seemed like he'd discovered new things while he'd been unconscious. That in those far-off places he had found the wisdom that comes with knowing your time is extremely limited.

'Hello, girl, how are ya?'

'Better than you,' I replied.

'Yep, I'd reckon so.' He laughed.

'Bloody hell, Uncle Hayd, what have you done?'

'Yeah, I know, girl. I know.'

'Can I get you anything?'

'I'd love another Coke Zero.'

'Yep, can do. Don't go anywhere while I'm gone, okay?'

'I'll see what I can do,' he replied with a smile.

I've never taken a request so seriously in my life – it became my mission. My sole purpose for existing in that moment was to find my uncle a Coke Zero. A simple task one would think, no?

No.

Do you think I could? Pepsi Max as far as the eye could see, but no Coke Zero.

As you can imagine, I became hysterical in the hospital cafeteria. I couldn't believe I was going to fail in his one request. I went over and asked the ladies at the information desk if there were any vending machines that sold Coke in the hospital. They must have thought me a mad woman – I was panting and sobbing all at once. They pointed me in the right direction and I set off once again, steadfast in my determination to locate the fucking Coke Zero. I found the machine ... COKE ZERO! Praise be! I got my crisp $50 note out, the one I had just withdrawn from the ATM – it was Haydn's special last request, and I wanted brand new money for some reason, only the best would do. Wait? What is this? The machine doesn't take notes? *Of course it fucking doesn't.*

I'm not ashamed to say I kicked the shit out of that machine. I refused to be defeated. I looked around for someone to swap money with, but there was not a soul to be seen.

In desperation I checked the change slot, and guess what I found?

Four bucks.

A Coke Zero was $3.70.

If I was a religious person, I'd say that was a sign.

I raced back up to my uncle and presented him with the Coke Zero, I put a straw in it, held it to his mouth and he drank the whole thing down in one go. I sat with him a bit longer and we chatted as we always did. I only saw him a few times a year but he and my aunty had always been great supporters of mine when most of the family had decided I was a pain in the arse.

I told him I loved him.

I thanked him for always having my back.

He looked at me and said something that broke and healed me all at once.

'You're a good girl, Em, always have been.'

I've always felt like the family screw-up, the joke, the black sheep, that I was never quite good enough for anyone. I was for him though and for me, finally, that was enough.

Then my Uncle Russ called me out of the cubicle and quietly told me that someone needed to go and tell my Nana Denise (the writer of the wedding synopsis and my favourite member of the family) that her beloved son was not going to make it.

That the news should not be delivered on the phone, and that she shouldn't be alone when she got it. Nana couldn't be there as she herself was in hospital, two hours away in Shepparton, unwell and unable to be moved. I volunteered for the job as I could tell everyone else was reluctant to leave Haydn's side. I also wanted to be the one to do it as my Nana and I were really tight, and I knew she'd prefer to hear it from me if she couldn't hear it from Uncle Russ.

As I was driving up the Hume Highway to be with my grandmother, I just couldn't believe what was happening. You see, my uncle had always seemed bulletproof to me, and the person I was going to see was his number one fan. My Nana had five kids and all of them would attest to the fact that Uncle Hayd was her favourite. He had stayed in the small country town they'd all been raised in when the others had made lives elsewhere. He looked after her, and was always just a phone call away should Nana need anything.

I arrived at the hospital, walked through her ward and, as I came around the corner, I saw her sitting in a wheelchair looking frail and worried. I stood still and watched her, knowing I was about to obliterate her life, and I wanted her to have a few more moments of a world where there was still a chance Haydn would make it.

She sensed my presence and called out to me, and as soon as she saw my face, she broke down.

I'd spent weeks driving back and forth to visit her in Shepparton, and we'd grown even closer over that time.

I'd been taking her spare nighties and underwear, and making sure she had fresh flowers and magazines. My Aunty Rachael had been doing the same, making the five-hour road trip from her place in Tumbarumba each week to take care of Nana. At this point I wish to acknowledge Rachael and the unbelievable selflessness she showed towards her mother.

When Haydn first had the accident I went to be with Nana on the Tuesday. She spoke non-stop about his strength and how she hoped it would all be okay. She also made me go over the accident time and time again – she wanted to be shown a map of where it had happened exactly. She asked several times who the person who stopped to help Alva had been. Did she know them? She craved details as the elderly so often do, and I did my best to fill in the gaps for her.

It was Friday now and I was there to tell her that it wasn't going to be okay.

I went to her and said how sorry I was. I desperately tried to hold back the tears as I held her. I wanted to be a source of strength for her – she was so fragile – I wanted her to feel as though she could lean into me. I remembered at that moment that she was a mother, a mother being told that her son was going to die. It didn't matter that she was eighty-one, you never stop being a mother and mothers aren't built to cope with the death of their children. That's not how nature intends it to be: we go first, not them.

There were other people in the room and above all things my Nana was a proud woman; I knew she would be mortified at crying in front of other people, so I busted her out of the ward. I put a blanket on her and wheeled her straight out the emergency exit and into a small garden area so that she could grieve in private. She asked me to call my Uncle Russ and ask if Haydn could speak on the phone so she could say goodbye to him.

Haydn was not strong enough to speak on the phone by that stage. Passing that information on to my grand-mother, that she would not be able to speak with her child one last time, was one of the single hardest moments of my life. After a short while, Nana asked to go back inside so she could sleep. Life had just become too much for her. Nana had chronic arthritis and fragile bones, so much so that moving her in and out of bed had fractured one of her arms. She could not be transported to see Haydn in Melbourne and he couldn't be moved either, and the phone call was her last hope.

On Saturday 18 October 2014, exactly a week after cele-brating his youngest son's marriage, Uncle Haydn passed away. With my Aunty Alva and Uncle Russ by his side.

He donated all his organs, except his eyes. Those impres-sive blue eyes. I'd want to take them with me too.

After Haydn's funeral my Nana started going downhill fast, her heart was broken and her will to live gone. Again I found myself in a hospital, watching the light leave someone very close to me. On New Year's Eve I was called away to work in Sydney, to host a broadcast covering the fireworks and festivities. We desperately needed the money and so after much thought I decided to do it; I'd be in and out in 24 hours. I didn't want to leave Nana, but I thought I had time. I now look back and wish I could take that decision back. I'm not sure I'll ever be able to forgive myself for leaving her. I kept close checks on her throughout the night and was told she didn't have long. I went to bed making so many deals with God, I bargained and pleaded. My phone rang at 6.32am and it was Aunty Rachael. I knew what it meant, but I didn't want to answer because then it would be real.

Denise Spence passed away on New Year's Day 2015, nine weeks after her son Haydn. With my Aunty Rachael and Uncle Russ by her side.

Again my family had one of its most beloved members ripped from it.

Just know Nana was a force of nature, a damn fine cook and hands down the funniest person I have ever known. I spent most summers with her as a kid, and besides my own mother, she was the single most important female influence in my life. She was my number one fan and I was hers.

To be perfectly frank, she wouldn't want you to know too much about her last few days, when she stopped putting on her lippy and worrying about her hair. That's when we knew things were really bad. My grandmother, no matter what, always 'put on her face'.

The eulogy I gave at her funeral probably best sums up my relationship with her. On the day I wore white and one of her brooches and painted my lips red in her honour. I now always wear red lips in her honour.

For Nana.

As far back as I can remember, Nana and I were great mates. Having both been blessed with the ability to talk underwater with paper bags on our heads and a matching set of harsh tongues, we would sit and chat for hours about, well, most of you, actually.

Our friendship was really only tested once when I was twelve years old. She had come down for the school holidays as she so often did, to look after my sister and I. On this one day we were about to start a marathon cooking session and needed to fire up our dodgy oven. It refused to spring to life, so Nana stuck her head in to investigate further and just at that moment I flicked a mystery switch and the oven roared to life, taking with it Nana's eyebrows and eyelashes – every last one. We subsequently spent the rest of the school holidays searching for a waterproof eyebrow pencil in the right shade of grey. She never really mastered drawing them on properly, in the end she had to grow the front of her silver perm slightly longer to cover the bald spots.

I know that I inherited Nana's resilience, independence and sense of humour. Nana made me laugh more than anyone else I know. Her sense of humour was about as dry as they come and her wit, razor sharp. No-one was safe from her assessment and judgement. I loved hearing about the weekly Scrabble sessions she had with her pals and the comings and goings at the church plant shop. I loved how harsh and cutting she could be. I always knew where things stood between us.

I'll miss her disapproving 'lips of string' and the waft of Elizabeth Arden's Red Door perfume from the bedroom before we'd go out to the big store. I'll miss her pinching my ear when I said something she didn't like and the way she would hold my hand and pick at my nails absentmindedly. It used to drive me crazy but now I'd give anything to have those weathered, arthritic fingers digging at mine.

She loved Downton Abbey *and had a delightful yet slightly disturbing love of Eddie McGuire.*

She was the queen of putting on a brave and glamorous face, no matter how bad things got, she always managed impeccable hair, red lipstick and a pair of kickarse shoes.

Sorry for saying 'arse' at your funeral, Nana.

Nana, who will iron my underwear and aggressively steam the crotch? She would do that, she would slam the iron down on top of them, never breaking eye contact with me, and say, 'You never know what's lurking here, Emelia.'

Who will call me Emelia?

Who will pray for me now and save me from eternal damnation?

She was my friend, my role model and my hero.

My world is a lesser place without her. I'll miss her, I miss her.

Go well, Nana. Go well.

She would have been so excited for you all to read about her, and to be in my book would be considered the highest of honours by her. She would have also wanted me to mention that she was a multiple blue-ribbon winner at the Country Women's Association bake-offs and royal shows, regularly attended the Anglican Church and that she once went to visit the Queen of England with my mother. I have popped a photo in the picture section, please note red beret, red jacket, red lipstick: the woman was a colour coordinating ANIMAL.

Bloody hell, I miss her.

So there you have it, the grief Olympics, starring my family.

I'm a bit broken and numb now, since I have written this all in one go. I knew that if I took a break it wouldn't get finished and now I'm not sure what to do with myself. I'm trying not to think about the things I have just written and have been completely consumed by it all the same.

The day of Nana's funeral I made a choice to go out and make that woman so fucking proud of me she'd have no choice but to come back and tell me so. Something snapped in me when I was standing at her grave (which was next to my uncle's) and I decided not to let their deaths define me. Not to let the sadness destroy me because I was close, I was dangerously on the edge that day. I really could have gone either way; the grief was warm and inviting,

250

it was begging me to give into it. These events truly have a way of slamming things into perspective, don't they? Those ridiculous inspiration quotes and photos about not taking anything for granted and living in the present start making sense. Telling those you care about that you in fact do care about them.

I have lost all my grandparents now; I was lucky enough to have them all for a long time.

Violanté (Nonna).

Edward (Grandfather Ted).

Luigi (Grandpa).

Denise (Nana).

I am a product of all of you, carrying many of your good and bad traits. I hope I'm making you all proud.

To my Uncle Haydn, the red-headed 6 foot 4 hole you left is still being felt, we all miss you.

Love,
Girl.

15

Dad is Psychic

*D*o you remember I promised I'd let you know what happened at the Oxfam comedy gala way back at the start of this crazy ride?

Now, where did we leave off? Ah, yes. Dad and I were about to walk out on stage and I was having a moment. Then my dear pal Joel Creasey introduced me. I looked at Dad and was momentarily struck by how far he and I had come. How just a few short years ago I'd been a single, unemployed mother living with him and Mum, borrowing petrol money to be able to drive the kids to school. And how as a kid I had sat with him and watched this very broadcast never imagining that we would be on it. How so many things had contributed to the person about to walk out on stage and perform in front of three thousand people.

Dad and I took to the stage. I was the second last performer of the evening and the crowd was exhausted. There had been roughly fifty-seven comics on before me and no alcohol consumed. I could feel they needed a lift, so I set about doing just that. I did my 'three promises I can make to people without children' bit and then sang my version of 'There are Worse Things I Could Do' from *Grease*. What did you say? You don't know those bits?

Yes okay, I will pop them in here so you can truly be on stage with us. So imagine Dad and me on the stage. He sits down on a stool as I stride out all guns blazing in the sensible red frock and announce: 'Hey bitches! I'm Em and this is my dad, Vincie, or as the internet calls us, "What the hell happened to Ruby Rose and Super Mario?" I have two children, one is eight and the other is thirteen and I love them equally, I just love one a little more equally than the other. One corrects my spelling, says I drink too much wine and knows everything, and the other one is eight.

'It's no secret that kids are disgusting. They are vile little things who will wipe their hands, noses and arses on pretty much anything. What they don't tell you before you have children is how low your own personal hygiene standards will drop.

'Where are the people in the crowd who are yet to spawn? Pop those hands up so I know whose tyres to spoke on the way out . . .

'There you all are. Well, as a parent, I feel it is my duty to warn you of the things that the pregnancy books don't tell you. I wish to make you all three solemn promises and if you look around you as I make them, I guarantee you'll see all the people who have children nodding aggressively in agreement.

'The first promise I want to make you is that one day, you will run towards projectile vomit. You will willingly hold out your hands to stem the tide of spew.

'The second promise I wish to make you is that one day you will have a top drawer full of human teeth and hair. I have taken that a step further and still have the peg with the top of my kid's umbilical cord attached. It looks like birth beef jerky!

'The final promise I wish to make you is that one day, without question, you will stand, clap and cheer as another human does a shit in front of you.

'That is what they should be teaching in Sex Ed at school. Don't get the kids to carry a raw egg like it's a baby. Get them to carry a steaming human turd around in an ice-cream container. That will lower teen pregnancy levels quick smart.

'But there are even worse things that we do.

'*There are worse things I could do, than to skip a page or two.*
Last night you wet my bed, I didn't change it, I didn't care, I slept on damp sheets, yes it's true, but there are worse things that I do.

I often lie about bedtime, that's not Ribena, it's red wine.
I encourage cheating, yes, so the game can finally end,
I licked your dummy clean it's true,
But there are worse things that I do.
I took a shit with you on my lap,
Caught your spew in my bare hands,
Picked out head lice, gave up dreams, shaved my legs with Sudocrem,
Dropped a fart and I blamed you.
I once forgot about you too, left you at the Melbourne Zoo.

'Thanks very much! I'm Em Rusciano and that is my dad, Vincie!'

After six hours of angst it was done! We got pretty big laughs and I felt okay after I came off. I mean, I'd left some things out and rushed a little, however I didn't hate what I'd delivered, which is always a bonus. Everyone was exhausted backstage, especially Joel, who had done an excellent job hosting the night. It was a marathon effort – considering he'd been away from civilisation, technology, the media and his family and friends for almost three months in the jungle, his performance was bloody impressive.

Dad and I packed up and drove home, and Dad dissected the performance as he always does in typical Vincie fashion.

'You could tell they're tired, we got them going but you could tell. Who was that fucking clown, Em? He was a bit morbid. You did well to come on after him. I think we need to speed "Worse Things" up a little. They liked the poo gags, everyone likes the poo gags. Wait till I tell the boys at golf, they won't believe that we played the Palais!'

That was the big payoff for Dad, bragging to the boys at golf that he'd made his Oxfam comedy gala debut at sixty-three years of age and done it at the majestic Palais Theatre!

About a week after the taping, the day that the gala was due to go to air, I received a phone call from my manager, Andrew. It was very early in the morning. I was instantly worried when I saw his number – in my experience, phone calls before 7am rarely bring good news.

'Hey, darlin'.'

'Hey, AT, what's up? Is everything okay?'

'Well, no. There is no easy way to tell you this but they've cut you from the gala broadcast tonight. Your spot won't go to air. I'm sorry, I think it's a stupid decision but it's completely out of my hands.'

'Oh. Oh, okay. Well. Did they say why? I mean, was I really bad? I thought it went okay. I need to know why, Andrew.'

'I don't know, just know that lots of people went to bat for you but ultimately politics got in the way, they needed to save time and you got cut. I'm really sorry, Em, I know you must be very disappointed.'

'It's okay. [Lump building in throat.] I'd better call Dad.'

I hung up and burst into tears, partly because I felt sorry for myself but mostly because I had to call Dad, who had told every single person he had come into contact with, including the guy who delivers his eBay packages, that he was going to be on the telly performing in the Oxfam comedy gala with his daughter. I didn't want to tell him, he had done so much for me and asked for so little in return. The fact I was able to give him this experience meant a lot to me and now it was being taken away for apparently unknown reasons. I felt rejected, humiliated and bitterly disappointed. All the old insecurities came bubbling up and unfortunately my husband got caught in the crossfire when he found me pacing the kitchen, partaking in some silent, angry crying.

'What's wrong?'

'Andrew called to say that Dad and I got cut from the gala broadcast tonight.'

'Oh, that's shit.'

'Yes, it is, thank you very much, Captain Obvious. And now I have to phone Dad and break it to him.'

'He'll be okay, he was just happy to be there with you. He doesn't care about that other stuff. It will be okay. Did Andrew say why you got cut?'

'No, he says he doesn't know why, he mentioned politics but didn't go into specifics.'

'Well, did you learn anything after your performance? Can you take anything away from this?'

'Fuck off with your unsolicited life coaching, Scott! I just need to feel sorry for myself for a bit, okay?'

Scott left the room and I sat down at the table and thought back to all the things that had happened in the lead-up to the gala. Would I have done anything differently? If I was being honest with myself, I would have done *everything* differently. I wouldn't have arrived six hours early, I would've stuck to my guns about my costume, I would've kept to myself, run my own race and not listened to the other comics chatting. I would've not drunk beer, I would've eaten something and I would've slowed down on stage. Look at all those lessons! Just look! That didn't take away the sting of being omitted from the line-up but it did make me feel like I'd taken something away from the experience.

So I called Dad and I told him that we'd been left off the list, and, as Scott predicted, he didn't care at all. He was just happy to have done it, in the moment, and didn't need the televised accolades as well.

'We've already sold out all our shows, Em, we don't need the publicity! And don't worry, because one day you'll play your own show there. On your terms. And I'll be there. I just know it.'

The very next week we began our assault on the Melbourne International Comedy Festival, twenty-three shows in a row with Mondays off. I'd already performed *The Motherload* in Adelaide and Perth to an overwhelmingly positive response so I knew we had something pretty great on our hands.

Here is the show blurb for those of you who missed it:

Imagine all the love of a Celine power ballad and all the snot and isolation of an Ebola outbreak.

This show's kinda like that clip Beyoncé did with Blue Ivy, only with more C-bombs, more references to extreme toilet paper usage and no attempt whatsoever to hide marital difficulties.

From parenting in the 80s to her hatred of the Disney musical Frozen, The Motherload *will leave no stone unturned, no relationship unexamined, no swear word unsworn.*

Oh and there will be a John Farnham singalong, by God, there will be John Farnham singalong. Accompanied by her long suffering father, Vincie, Em will rip through your heart like herpes at a Blue Light Disco. If you've had a mother, then this show is for you.

The reviews were pretty awesome as well.

'Em Rusciano is an irrepressible force of nature. ★★★★★'
RIP IT UP

'Rusciano delivers some of the best written, outrageously funny comedy I've ever witnessed with near perfect precision.' *Same Same*

'Solid, rhinestone-studded gold.' *The Age*

It could not have gone better. The week after my Nana passed away was the week I began touring this show, and I threw myself into work. As you now know, it sold out and went on to be a roaring success, so much so I was able to buy a house. A whole house, for Scotty and the girls and I to live in. Flashback to that broken mess in Perth who had to sell everything up and thought she'd destined her family to a life poverty and gloom, and you may understand the importance of that fact. The day the real estate agent handed over the keys (fun fact: his brother was the one I fake dated in high school to get close to my real crush Ryan), I burst into tears.

I don't know if I believe in guardian angels but I have had some seriously good career and life luck since my beloved Nana left me. She was totally down with the Gee Oh Dee. God and her were tight, so I have some pretty impressive weight in my corner. I speak to her and Uncle Haydn before I go on stage anywhere, I see him standing in a stream fishing and I see her sitting in a chair, adjusting her brooch and clutching her handbag. I always keep two seats empty for them at every show. No one knows that – except you now.

I have just finished touring *Em Rusciano is NOT a Diva*, which I hope many of you saw. I decided to step it up a notch and include a band; Dad was still involved but he deserved some back up. Rob Mills put me in touch with a great music director, Jeremy, who I happened to go to school with, and Jeremy found me a family. I know that's gross but it's true. I'd been touring on my own for so long that having the boys to hang out with before and after the shows was a revelation. It's lonely doing stand-up; once you get off stage the silence can be deafening and all consuming. Marcel, Fab, Kim, Jeremy and Dad kept me going, made me sound amazing and taught me a great deal about being a musician.

The most exciting thing about this tour was the venue we played the Melbourne shows in. Can you even begin to guess where I did my very own solo show for the 2016 Melbourne International Comedy Festival?

YEP! THE FUCKING PALAIS THEATRE, BITCHES!

Remember what Dad said a couple of pages back? After we'd been cut from the gala? I'll remind you so you don't have to turn back through the book because: annoying.

'We've already sold out all our shows, Em, we don't need the publicity! And don't worry, because one day you'll play your own show there. On your terms. And I'll be there. I just know it.'

How right he had been, and almost exactly a year to the day!

I spent a lot of the two shows just watching Dad; he was loving it – and himself – sick. All his golf buddies came, my mum came, my cousins Dave and Tom came – it was the best concert I had ever given for my family! If you'd have told eight-year-old Em after she had given a thrilling performance in the kitchen to 'I Touch Myself' by The Divinyls that she would one day be on stage in a similar outfit in front of three thousand people who actually wanted to be there and who were not her dolls and family members, she would have said –

Look, to be honest, she would have said, 'Duh, obviously I know, have you seen how good I am?' And then she would have done an aggressive body roll and high kicked out of the room.

16

A Just-in-Case-of-Death Letter to My Daughters

To the brilliant Marchella and the magnificent Odette. You may or may not know this, but since you were born I've had a rather morbid tradition of writing you each a letter before I go away in case something happens to me on said trip. Since someone has been kind enough to let me write a book, I thought I could pop a letter in here to be preserved for all of time. So now you won't have to rummage through my filing cabinet only to find food wrappers, old photos and library fines. Hopefully now, when you find yourselves in a jam, you can flick open this very page and here I'll be with some posthumous words of wisdom. Know that I didn't want to leave you, that my last

265

thought would've been of the both of you. You are the most impressive thing I've ever done, my greatest achievement, the loves of my life (besides your father, of course). Look after your dad. Was his shirt ironed at my funeral? Was I carried out to Kylie Minogue's 'Your Disco Needs You' as instructed?

Even though I'm not physically there you both still carry me under your skin, in the shape of your eyes and the freckles across your noses. In your dry and slightly sick senses of humour, in your love of all things shiny and in your huge, hobbit toes. There I'll be, never far, always connected to you.

Be sassy, kind-hearted, fierce bitches. Pick great friends who contribute to your experience as a human. Ditch the drainers and the drama queens. You've so many better things to do than be tortured by unhappy people. Don't take shit from anyone, ever. I really mean that. Don't be afraid to say NO. No is your friend. Don't ever put the fear of offending someone in front of your own personal safety – emotional and physical. Having said all that, say YES as often as you can! Yes to new experiences, yes to the unknown, YES TO LIFE.

In summary: NO to the dickheads and YES to the legends!

Look after your body. Nourish it, water it and exercise it. If you do all that then you will never have to worry about the thin/fat/broken scenarios. Praise it, reward it, don't ever view it as something less than. You two have such magnificent, strong bodies that can do so many impressive things.

Have the courage to tell each other the truth when one of you asks, 'How are you?' If the answer is 'not great' then say that. If you get that answer from your sister, then ask her, 'How can I help?'

Start working on building a safe place inside of you, somewhere to retreat when the world becomes too loud. A place to belong that feels like home, so that no matter where you are in the world you have that space. You'll have to be kind to yourselves to be able to build this magical haven. This isn't a strong point for the women in our family, but I'm confident you two can do it.

Don't worry about getting married, that whole notion is a crock of shit. Little girls are conditioned to believe that marriage is the end game, the final goal. It just isn't, it is an option along the line should you choose it. I've been drilling that into you both since you were little girls but if I'm gone too soon, before the brainwashing is complete, highlight this section and reread it often. Whomever you end up with, just make sure that they challenge you, admire you and respect you and want to be your friend as well as your lover. That last part can't be too far one way or the other. If you choose a life dedicated to food, travel and dogs then I'm sure that will be just as enriching as any other path.

When you find yourself on the precipice of a complete emotional breakdown ask yourself the following questions:

1. Am I tired?
2. Have I eaten enough?
3. Am I thirsty?
4. When did I last exercise?
5. What is coming up for me that I'm worried about?

Then sit down and have a hot drink and ninety per cent of the time you will feel better. If by chance you are in that ten per cent where the above list and a hot drink isn't helping, call your sister and tell her. Talk it through. You should also talk to your dad. He is *very* good in these situations. He is excellent at preventing the world from caving in around you. (I'm speaking from experience here. At times, his extreme stoicism is all that kept me sane.) Failing your sister and your father, go and seek professional help. I cannot stress that enough: therapy is a very, very good thing. Find yourself a good head doctor and you will be okay, I promise. I spent my life overthinking things, trying to control the outcome of situations so as to avoid any pain. It is a terrible burden and it corroded my insides. I do not wish that for either of you.

Look after yourself. Never expect anyone to provide for you. Earn your own cash, find your own path, be in control of the things that happen to you. Find out what it is that makes you happy and try to make a living doing that. Don't accept a job you hate just for the money, that will destroy your soul and end badly, trust Mummy on that one. Call your dad three times a week when you move out, family is important. *Our family* is important.

Go to the library often, and keep reading. You both currently love books; even though screens are calling your names, against all odds, you still respect the page. Books don't run out of batteries and you can't crack or break them. Volunteer, help out those who are less fortunate than you. It's just a good thing to do and on a selfish level it helps for when you get too far into your own head. Volunteering allows you to get outside of yourself, it has a way of putting life back into focus when it becomes blurry and illegible.

Keep your pubic hair, trim it at the sides so as to adhere to some form of social expectations but keep most of it. Leave your eyebrows alone, Mummy went too far down the nineties path and had to draw them on for the rest of time. That added at least fifteen minutes to my morning schedule – you saw the work I had to put into them! Buy the best underwear you can afford, cotton ones: your vagina needs to breathe. If things go wrong down south go see a doctor straightaway. White pants don't suit anyone, invest in great jeans and *never*, under any circumstances, wear plastic bra straps in lieu of a strapless bra. Everyone can see them, they're not a cloak of invisibility, adding diamantés to them does not improve them! Besides spitting on my grave and insulting my legacy you will just look like a bedazzled rack of lamb. Hold off on cutting a fringe, you might think you want to but it only looks good for a week and then you spend a year trying to grow it out, just go and buy a clip-on one should the mood strike.

Find yourself a gay or five, gay men are your friends, it's in both your DNA to be attracted to them. You can't turn them, believe me, but you can love them and they will love you back just as fiercely. I bequeath you Michael and Lyndon, they will now field your pop culture, relationship and fashion-related questions. The two of them combined basically makes me so it will be like I'm still there.

Try not to spend too much time watching boys do stuff, make sure you get out and do your own shit. Make music, play sport, build things, write; do it yourself. Don't be relegated to a spectator.

Be each other's strength, you're such a complementary pair. Odie the smiling, crafty, wheeler dealer and Chella always measured, cautious and sensible. Chella, remember to stay in the light, avoid overthinking things and trust your gut. Stay close to your sister and you will always be okay, Odette brings the sunshine into room, the light seems to follow her wherever she goes. Odie, don't do too much stupid shit, okay? I love you dearly, my wonderful baby, however sometimes you go where the wind takes you, which isn't always the best place! Maybe just run any major life decisions by Chella and Dad before making them.

Stay away from ice, the drug not frozen water. It is an insidious beast that is taking hold of many people I know and once it finds its way into your veins and bloodstream it becomes nearly impossible to defeat. I accept you may try other forms of illegal substances but you must make a solemn DEATH vow that ice will not be one of them. Same goes for heroin and LSD. Look, I would prefer if you didn't try *anything*, drugs are bad. Just say no, okay?

Odie, you're a colourful, clever, wondrous human; never lose that magic.

Chella, you're brave, funny and smart; don't ever doubt yourself for a minute.

You've both got this and by 'this' I mean life.

I love you both to the moon and back times infinity.

(Remember to avenge me should I have gone out in mysterious circumstances.)

Love,

Mum

Self Help with Me: Em Rusciano!

Well done! You made it to the end of my written self-indulgence, how are you feeling? Do you need a shower? A wine? A sedative?

Me too.

I guess this is the part of the book where I tell you what I've learned, where I provide the silver bullet to happiness and fulfilment, a succinct summary for you to put in your pocket and live your best life with.

Sorry, you guys, I can't do that – I'm not Oprah.

Yet.

I do feel some sort of responsibility that you at least get something useful from my book other than my inability to track my menstrual cycle, visions of my hirsute lower half and a handy guide on how not to crash a funeral, so the following will be the 'self-help' portion of the book. On the subject of the self-help book I wish to say, dear reader: NEVER EVER BUY THOSE BOOKS!

[*Editor's note: Em, we have many respected authors in this genre, can you please rework this sentence?*]

Look, I'm sure there are maybe two good self-help bibles and if you really benefit from them, great, who am I to tell you to stop? I just feel there are a lot of opportunistic vultures out there who write these books filled with empty, new-age bullshit that prey on the overweight, lonely and clinically depressed, and deliver nothing more than some inspirational memes and a step-by-step guide to blaming yourself. These chirpy morons are *cashing in* big time – we're spending in the billions per year on this crap.

[*Ed: Okay, I think that is actually more offensive; let's just keep it as it was.*]

Parenting!

(I hope the use of the exclamation marks makes this subject seem friendly and approachable. Imagine me in sensible slacks, crocs and a skivvy if that helps.)

As some of you know, being a small person's legal guardian can be equal parts ball-tearingly frustrating and gut-wrenchingly exhilarating. It can take your breath away and have you questioning all you hold dear in the space of ten minutes. I don't profess to be an expert on the topic,

I readily admit that on occasion my kids eat cereal for dinner and wear bathers for undies, and yet I get asked about parenting at least once a day. The following is a handy guide to the things I feel are important when raising young people.

Let me stress that I'm *not* a parenting expert, I'm the opposite of that, so . . . a parenting moron? No, that doesn't seem right.

Em's ten thoughts on parenting

1. Tell your kid when they stuff up.
Real-life example: 'Odette, putting my mobile phone in the microwave was a bonehead thing to do. Can you please tell me why you felt that was okay because I am here to tell you – it so wasn't.'

2. Tell your kid it is okay to stuff up.
Real-life example: 'I accept you were trying to do a scientific experiment to ascertain if phones melt, I love that you were interested in finding out the truth. Having a crack at stuff is great, just ask me first because: giant electrical fire.'

3. Speak to them how you want them to speak to you.
I have really had to work on this one, mainly because 'sarcastic bitch' is my default setting. If your kids are being rude little arsehats, it may be time to look at how you relate to them. I did and things have taken on a much gentler tone in my house.

4. Get down on the floor with them.

We're all guilty of remote-control parenting but kids bloody love it when you get down on their level; it allows you to fully engage. I know it seems like a punishment at the time but I promise, five minutes into building Barbie's dream house you will be all about Ken's den and the curtains in the day room.

5. Give them good food.

This one is so important. I know sometimes it can be tough and fast food is easy, you just need to think about all the chemicals, sugar and crap you are pumping into your small person's body. If you teach them good food habits early they will always have them. My parents did and for that I am extremely grateful. At the time I resented the home-cooked, market-fresh wog food. All I wanted was a packet of Twisties, a Vegemite sandwich and a Prima. My parents maintained the rage and as a result I have pretty good eating habits. My kids will too.

6. Read them good books.

Recommendation: *Don't Let the Pigeon Drive the Bus* is perfect for all ages. It is the best children's book almost ever. In fact, anything by Moe Willams is super rad, he appeals to all ages.

7. Teach them the importance of actual gratitude.

I don't go in for this 'I'm a mum, it's just what we do' business. Who says that? Who says that as mothers we wipe shit up, work, cook, drive, clean, drive, drive, drive, because we're programmed to do so out of some kind of natural maternal instinct that kicks in the moment they pop out?

Bullshit.

I think some children believe that it is in their mother's DNA to love soaking their skiddy jocks, ironing their shirts and baking the entire class gluten-, nut-, wheat-, dairy- and taste-free cakes for the fete. Sorry, dickheads, it isn't.

(I'm sure your child isn't a dickhead, I just got a bit caught up, forgive me.)

Alls I'm saying is make sure they thank you for all that you do and *mean it*!

8. Pick them up when they fall.

Emotionally, physically and spiritually. Be there. Kids need to feel safe in order to be smart-brave. Smart-brave: I'm going to try this new thing without fear and do my best and if I fail I know I'm still loved.

9. If you fuck up, admit it and try again tomorrow. Kids forgive and forget in the blink of an eye.

Kids almost see it as a novelty when you admit to making a mistake. It is good for them to see that even Mum and Dad screw things up occasionally.

10. Love them till it hurts and then a little bit more.

That's it, nothing new or groundbreaking here. I tried to keep it simple, concise and devoid of wankery. I believe that parenting gets overcomplicated a lot of the time and I know we are all guilty of comparing ourselves to other parents and feeling as though we come up short. Some of us only post the highlight reel on Facebook – our children beautifully groomed and our houses immaculate – when in reality that shit took three hours to set up. I, like most of you, am doing my best to raise kids who contribute to the world. Kids who are kind to animals and those who are most vulnerable in society. The important part to remember is, you've got this. If you yell at your kid to make yourself feel better, that's okay – you've got this. Refer to number nine on my list then do number ten. See how it works! There is room for forgiveness and improvement, two crucial ingredients when trying to parent. Sometimes we get it gloriously right and sometimes the children are still awake at 10pm with no food for lunches and no clean uniforms.

Relationships!

There is no way to sugar-coat this: healthy relationships are fucking hard work. Times that by infinity if you decide to get married.

It is hinted at, written about, studied and mumbled, but I don't think enough married people are saying to other married people, 'My relationship can be a clusterfuck of disappointment, frustration and finger pointing.'

Which reminds me. Hey, you guys: Sometimes my marriage is a clusterfuck of disappointment, frustration and finger pointing.

(I really love the word clusterfuck. It is powerful, heavy and desperate all at once.)

There are thousands upon thousands of relationship experts giving us unsolicited advice on how to spice up our marriages, listen to our partners and generally have a dream union. No-one mentions what to do when you're in an epic stand-off with your other half over whose turn it is to clean up the dog's spew. 'Not mine!' you each declare, so the aforementioned spew sits for days, congealing on the bathroom floor into a circle of stiffened yellow stomach lining. That is the shit that tests marriages more than anything, the battle over whose turn it is to do the crappy menial everyday tasks. At least it is in my house. Add kids, and your life becomes about existing not living, you just get through days rather than experiencing them.

My *biggest* gripe with my family is the amount of work I do to keep us going vs the amount they contribute. When I get sick, which isn't often, my contribution to the machine that is our household stops for a few days. Cue the wheels falling off the entire operation. I resent this, I resent that the dickheads in my family can't seem to pick up the slack for two days, that the washing gets to an offensive level, there is no food and the house looks as though we are squatting in it.

Inevitably I will crack it with Scott. Our arguments usually involve me being disappointed with his lack of effort and him feeling ripped off and thinking that I choose to see the glass as half empty when it comes to him. He says I am too hard on him and that my standards are unrealistic – and he's totally right. You didn't see that one coming, did you? In response to my accusations he usually says, 'I did enough, everything is okay.' Yes it was, but not my version of okay. When I ask him to do something what I mean to say is 'Please do that thing *exactly* the way I would do it.' I like to scrub the toilet bowl until it cries for mercy; his version of that is flushing it and lighting a match.

Don't even get me started on the toilet roll war. Call me crazy, but I don't call placing the new roll *on top* of the holder doing it right!

Serenity now. Serenity now.

I share this with you because I want you to know that my marriage can be hard work. I feel that if more of us admitted that to each other, there'd be less pressure to be in a perfect relationship to begin with. We'd stop holding each other to unrealistic standards. Maybe you aren't going on romantic date nights like so many therapists recommend but maybe you got through the day without flipping the love of your life your middle finger while silently mouthing 'go fuck yourself sideways' and you're both lying silently on the couch together holding hands.

Cute.

My relationship can also be the bedrock upon which I build my emotional foundations. After losing Nana and Uncle Hayd, I'm pretty sure I would have folded in two and given up if it wasn't for my husband's support. I love him, he loves me, we love our kids and sometimes that breaks my balls and sometimes it makes my heart burst with joy.

It's not always bad, but it can be and that's all I really wanted to say.

Single?!

Okay, I am just gonna lay this one out fast and loose because I *know* you are over the avalanche of information out there for single people.

When confronted with a potential romantic situation, choose wisely, don't *resist* it or *assist* it, just let it happen. No game playing, no dating rules, no deep analysis – just let it be. Expectation usually leads to disappointment.

Also, and this is the IMPORTANT PART: *Say what you mean* and *mean what you say.* Then there can be no confusion, about anything.

So in summary:

1. Choose wisely.
2. Let it happen naturally.
3. Be honest.
4. Expect nothing.

Go into every new romantic situation with this intent. It puts you back in control, you will have the hand (as explained to us by George Costanza), you will hold the power of Grayskull.

Self-acceptance!

I am about to throw a question at you and I want you to absolutely, no-fooling answer it truthfully. Be honest with me.

How much time do you spend thinking about how you look?

Sticking to the rules of the game and not hiding anything, I shamefully admit that I think about my appearance about eighty per cent of the time and I'm bloody sick of it. I estimate I vow to start a new diet three or four times a week. This usually coincides with me not fitting into a dress, seeing myself in an unflattering light or trolling my friends' Facebook photos and thinking how much better they look than me. If I come anywhere near a reflective surface I scrutinise what I see.

The thing is, I'm not really sure who I am trying to look perfect for. It's as though I think I have a team of hot people following my every move *Big Brother*-style and any time I slip up physically they will announce it to the world. Obviously, I don't, and it is high time I got over myself. I did some research (read: typed 'what percentage of women are unhappy with their appearance' into Google) and found one study that said ninety-seven per cent of women in the UK were not happy with themselves physically. NINETY-SEVEN FECKING PER CENT!

I know that most ladies have areas on their bodies they would like to improve – we all know the trauma of going shopping for bathers and jeans – but I'm not sure many of us actually examine how much time we're spending thinking about these things and why we do it. Who do you want to look good for? I can't answer that, I don't know why I torture myself over the wobbly bit of skin around my belly button that occurred after childbirth. I'm not quite sure whose approval I am looking for – are you? Is there a Holy Grail of optimum hotness that, once reached, the voice of God bellows, 'Nailed it!' and then we can go and eat a pack of Tim Tams and be done with the relentless pursuit of perfection? I am exhausted, wrung out and defeated by the constant stream of bile my brain dishes out to my body. I am still embarrassed to have admitted to you how much time I spend thinking about how I look, but it needed to be done. I think of all the other purposeful and positive things I could have been doing with that brainpower instead of the punishing body-hate vortex I've had it caught up in.

Does any of this ring true for you? Perhaps I am the only one who has been spending a ridiculous amount of energy giving myself a hard time about the way I look. I'll accept that, but I highly doubt it.

So I went in search of ways to improve on this and found a 'helpful' list on *wikiHow* called:

HOW TO BE MORE CONFIDENT WITH THE WAY YOU LOOK (FOR GIRLS).
1. *Look at yourself in the mirror every day and say one positive thing about yourself.*
Em, you have very straight teeth.

2. Reward yourself with chocolate.
Say what? Really? This will help me improve my negative self-talk?! Consider it done!

3. Go for a relaxing walk around the mall.
Are you shitting me? Have you been to one of those places recently? Screaming children, harassed parents . . . I am pretty sure that is where the impending zombie apocalypse is beginning and is slowly spreading as we speak. I think you got this one wrong, *wikiHow.*

4. Be happy. Even someone gorgeous looking, when sad, is not attractive.
Really? I'm pretty sure that if Miranda Kerr pouted with sad eyes she'd look sultry and sexy and I'd just look like a maniacal idiot standing next to her smiling.

5. Go for a new look.
Dude! I am trying to love my current look that is why we are here!

Okay, so *wikiHow* wasn't all that helpful, but I am determined to spend less time thinking about my thighs and more time on my Harry Potter erotica fan fiction.

Yes, I write Harry Potter erotica fan fiction.

As if that surprises you!

TRUTH-BOMB ALERT: I didn't want to include the part about me being an elite junior athlete in this book, however it was just such a huge part of my life from the ages of six to eighteen and played such an important role in shaping the person I am today, that it felt wrong not to. I've been thinking about why I was so reluctant to write about it, to go back there, and I think it's because I feel as though it didn't pan out as I think it should have. I fell into a deep depression after my career ended due to my own stupidity. This whole book could have been dedicated to my love of track and field, it really was all I thought about and how I spent the majority of my time. Looking back, I didn't know how good I was, I didn't appreciate that I had some pretty special skills, I just remember always being super hard on myself and looking towards the next goal. I won state champs after state champs and never stopped to think, *Well done, mate, that's pretty ace.* I wish someone would've nailed me down and made me feel some pride. I never felt good enough, and I had a burning desire to prove some imaginary force wrong about me. Perhaps that was part of my drive. I may not have got as far as I did had I felt comfortable with who I was as a person.

Fuck, I need a rest. I'm very upset writing this, I'm just going to type what is happening for me now and see where we go. I feel extremely sad for that little girl, for young teenage Em who broke herself trying to prove herself. She was lonely, strung out and hollow a lot of the time but bloody capable. She was the queen of putting on a brave face, she very rarely failed. When she did, she came down so hard on herself, she would actually punish herself. She would deny her body food for days. Her wonderful body that gave her so much, and she punished it on a regular basis. She had the most awful, internal dialogue too. She regularly told herself she was useless, slow and, yep, not good enough.

Okay, I'm sobbing now. Jesus, I hope my publishers have put aside some serious cash for therapy, this is ripping open wounds I didn't even know I had.

Thus ends the self-help portion of the book, I hope you got something out of it!

[Insert picture of a kitten]
(*Editor's note: Em, you do not have the budget for so many photos as you have already exceeded the maximum amount allowed for your page and word count. Your request for a sealed and fold-out section could not be accommodated either.*)

So that's it, I'm sobbing as I write this because it means I did it, I got to the end of this fantastically exhausting and rewarding thing that I set out to write. (Yes, dear reader, as you've probably now established, I cried many, *many* times writing this thing that you've almost finished reading. How do you feel I've gone? Can you flick me a tweet or a FB post or an email when you get to this part please? I'd like your feedback . . . Only if it's nice. Ha! Seriously though, go do it right now.)

Thank you for reading my words, I hope you laughed, and I'm sorry if you cried. I'm so glad we found each other. Connecting with other like-minded people is the reason my career got a bit of a boost. I also put in a shitload of hard work but at its core, finding my crew and giving them the good stuff enabled me to begin building a career that I really love. To do all those things I told Scotty I wanted to do way back in 2011 after I'd left Perth and had to start again.

Writing this book has forced so much reflection. I've spent the twelve years since competing in *Australian Idol* furiously working, my head has been down for so long I forgot to look up and around. I've been my own worst enemy at times, I realise that now. If a friend of mine were to lay out the things I've accomplished over the past decade and refused to acknowledge or celebrate them, as I am prone to do, I would actually slap them. I guess I'm afraid that if I stop to roll around in a little bit of success, the universe will punish me for being so smug and throw some lightning my way. I somehow got in my head that acknowledging success meant that I would no longer strive to achieve it, that it would trigger a tidal wave of pent-up laziness in me. I want you to know I'm just having these epiphanies as I type these words.

Fuck, I need a drink.

Wait! Is that the sentiment I want to end the book on? Probably not. How about I just leave you with my favourite quote from Teddy Roosevelt? Yes, I know that usually happens at the start of the book but stuff it, why start playing by the rules now?

Thanks bitches, from the bottom of my black heart – thanks.

Spend yourself in a worthy cause and get in that arena. (That will make sense once you read the quote.)

Your pal,

Em x

It is not the critic who counts; not the man who points out how the strong man stumbles, or where the doer of deeds could have done them better. The credit belongs to the man who is actually in the arena, whose face is marred by dust and sweat and blood; who strives valiantly; who errs, who comes short again and again, because there is no effort without error and shortcoming; but who does actually strive to do the deeds; who knows great enthusiasms, the great devotions; who spends himself in a worthy cause; who at the best knows in the end the triumph of high achievement, and who at the worst, if he fails, at least fails while daring greatly, so that his place shall never be with those cold and timid souls who neither know victory nor defeat.

Theodore Roosevelt

Acknowledgements

Thanks to my kids for being epic humans, I love you both big time, you sexy jerks. Marchella, you frighten me with your brilliance, if I wasn't at the actual birth I would question if you were mine. Odie, you glorious kook. You're kind, smart and creative. You're an absolute joy. I'm so glad you picked me to be your mum. To my long suffering husband, Scotty, if we're still together when this goes to print – thanks for all your support and gentle encouragement. Sixteen years together is nothing to be sniffed at. I love your guts. If we're not, I get the dogs. (Fun fact: we split up after I wrote this bit, spent six months apart and are now back together. I'll tell you about it all in the next book.)

To Toby Dog, you're my favourite, always have been, always will be.

Roy Boy, we love you too obviously but you need to stop pissing inside, we're all sick of it. Lucky you're literally the cutest dog in the world.

To my dad, Vincie, thank you for coming out of retirement and giving me a career. But mostly thanks for letting me be who I am. You've always had my back, you taught me about loyalty and hard work, and I appreciate all that you've done for me. Thank you also for being a certifiable lunatic, I am what I am (good and bad) because of you.

To my mum, Jen, you're always there to catch me in a crisis. I'd have smashed into a thousand pieces by now if it weren't for you, so thank you.

To Lyndon, my husband of the fabulous variety, you're all a girl could ever want in life. You're also my go-to should I ever need to dump a dead body.

To Michael Lucas, I love you big time, bitch. You're my moral compass and life partner in every way except the sex stuff, obviously. Scott says thank you for sharing the burden of me, seriously, he just yelled that out.

Big ups to Andrew Taylor, Molly Taylor, Julie Lawless, Jeff Green and Heather Tyas who manage my work life. Yes, it takes that many people to control this situation. You can't be suprised. You guys are a pleasure to work with and make my job very easy, thank you.

Special thanks to Janelle Koenig.

Acknowledgements

To my editors Larissa, Bert and Kylie, and my fabulous publisher Dan – bitches, you refined this pile of tangled thoughts and words into something that won't get us sued! You allowed me to re-write it right up to the death knock, thank you for not breaking my balls. I wanted to get everything just right because books are forever.

I did it.

It's done now.

I can stop typing.

I am stopping.

Now.

I am crying.

Again.

Now I am laughing. So the real quote I am going to end the book on is one from Dolly Parton's character in *Steel Magnolias*, which seems far more appropriate for me than ending on Teddy Roosevelt (yes, this is the second reference to that film. It's one of my absolute favourites). Take it away Dolly!

'Laughter through tears is my favourite emotion.'

Services and Help

beyondblue

If you want to find out more about the signs and symptoms of depression and anxiety, treatments and where to get support, visit the beyondblue website at beyondblue.org.au or contact the beyondblue support service on 1300 22 4636.

Lifeline

Lifeline provides 24/7 crisis support and suicide prevention services. Visit lifeline.org.au or call 13 11 14.

Qlife

Australia's first national counselling and referral service for Lesbian, Gay, Bisexual, Transgender and Intersex (LGBTI) people provides a place to talk about mental health, relationships, isolation, coming out, discrimination and more. Phone counselling and web chat is available 3pm – 12am Australia-wide, seven days a week. Visit qlife.org.au or call 1800 184 527.

Kids Helpline

Australia's only free, 24/7 phone and online counselling service for young people aged 5 to 25. Go to kidshelpline. com.au or call 1800 55 1800.